SUCCESS

IS A JOURNEY

MAKE YOUR LIFE A
GRAND ADVENTURE

BRIAN TRACY

Executive Excellence Publishing
1344 East 1120 South
Provo, Utah 84606
phone: (801) 375-4060
fax: (801) 377-5960
web: www.eep.com
e-mail: custserv@eep.com

Ordering Information
Individual Sales: Executive Excellence Publishing products are available through most bookstores. They can also be ordered directly from Executive Excellence at the address above.

Quantity Sales: Executive Excellence Publishing products are available at special quantity discounts when purchased in bulk by corporations, associations, libraries, and others, or for college textbook/course adoptions. Please write to the address above or call Executive Excellence Publishing Book Sales Division at 1-800-304-9782.

Orders for U.S. and Canadian Trade Bookstores and Wholesalers: Executive Excellence Publishing books and audiotapes are available to the trade through LPC Group/Login Trade. Please contact LPC at 1436 West Randolph Street, Chicago, IL 60607, or call 1-800-626-4330.

First edition
Printed in the United States of America
10 9 8 7 6 5 4 3 2   03 02 01 00 99

ISBN 1-890009-49-0

Also available on audio: ISBN 1-890009-50-4

DEDICATION

To Christina, a great adventurer of the heart and mind.
You have come so far and done so well, and you have so many
wonderful experiences ahead of you. I am so proud of you.

THE PATTERN OF SUCCESS

TABLE OF CONTENTS

DON'T QUIT

When things go wrong, as they sometimes will,
When the road you're trudging seems all uphill,
When funds are low and the debts are high,
And you want to smile, but you have to sigh,
When care is pressing you down a bit,
Rest, if you must, but don't you quit.

Life is queer with its twists and turns,
As every one of us sometimes learns,
And many a failure turns about,
When he might have won had he stuck it out;
Don't give up though the pace seems slow,
You may succeed with another blow.

Success is failure turned inside out,
The silver tint of the clouds of doubt,
And you never can tell how close you are,
It may be near when it seems so far;
So stick to the fight when you're hardest hit,
It's when things seem worst that you must not quit.

—Author Unknown

CAUTION: THIS BOOK WILL CHANGE YOUR LIFE

You are about to embark on an exciting journey of exploration into the depths of the most fascinating person you will ever know: yourself.

Life is a journey, and every part of life is a small journey, complete in itself. You begin with a destination, either clear or fuzzy, travel with the inevitable ups and downs, and you finally arrive at your destination, which may or may not be what you had in mind. Your experiences along the way, and how you react to them, are what make you who you are and determine who you will become.

The more experiences you have, and the more you learn from them, the faster you become all you are capable of becoming. The bad news is, we tend to learn more from the mistakes and detours than we do from the miles of smooth road. The good news is we can have Brian Tracy as our traveling companion.

You have extraordinary intelligence, talent, ability, and skill that you can develop and direct toward accomplishing exceptional things and making a real difference in the world. This book will show you how to tap into them.

I've known Brian Tracy for several years. He is one of the most respected speakers and consultants in America, and perhaps the world. (I ought to know; we've shared the platform on several occasions, and I've sat in the first row taking notes.) His books, articles, audio and video programs, and seminars have been published in 31 countries, in 18 different languages. Brian has the unique ability to draw timeless truths and principles from his experiences, and then share them with others in such a clear and simple way that their lives and thinking are changed forever.

Everyone wants to be successful. Everyone wants to be healthy and happy, do meaningful work, and achieve financial independence. Everyone wants to make a difference in the world, to be significant, to have a positive impact on those around him or her. Everyone wants to do something wonderful with his or her life.

Luckily for most of us, success is not a matter of background, intelligence, or native ability. It's not our family, friends, or contacts who enable us to do extraordinary things. Instead, it is our ability to get the very best out of ourselves under almost all conditions and circumstances. It is *your* ability, as Theodore Roosevelt said, to "Do what you can with what you have, right where you are."

The great success formula has always been the same. First, decide exactly what you want and where you want to go. Second, set a deadline and make a plan to get there. (Remember, a goal is just a dream with a deadline.) Third, take action on your plan; do something everyday to move toward your goal. Finally, resolve in advance that you will persist until you succeed, that you will never, ever give up.

This formula has worked for almost everyone who has ever tried it. It is simple, but not easy. It will require the very most you can give and the best qualities you can develop. In developing and following this formula, you will evolve and grow to become an extraordinary person.

One more thing: Learn from the experts. You will not live long enough to figure it all out for yourself. And what a waste it would be to try, when you can learn from others who have gone before. Ben Franklin once said, "Men can either buy their wisdom or they can borrow it from others. The great tragedy is that most men prefer to buy it, to pay full price in terms of time and treasure."

Over and over, I have found that a single piece of information, a single idea at the right time, in the right situation, can make all the difference. I have also learned that the great truths are simple. They are not found in complex formulas that require a rocket scientist to interpret. The great truths are contained in basic ideas and principles that virtually anyone can understand and apply. Your greatest goal in life should be to acquire as many of them as possible and then use them to help you do the things you want to do and become the person you want to become.

Before you start reading this book, fasten your seat belt; it's a real page-turner. As you join Brian and his friend, Geoff, on their journey, and face the challenges they face, you will find yourself learning about life at a more rapid rate than you may have thought possible. You will see yourself and your own story in almost every page.

As Brian says, "Everyone has a Sahara to cross." You and I move in and out of crises on a regular basis. The turbulence and turmoil of life are inevitable and unavoidable. The only part of the equation you control is how you respond. As Epictetus, the Roman philosopher, once said, "Circumstances do not make the man; they merely reveal him to himself."

At the end of this book, you will be a different person, a better person, a wiser person. In fact, you may never be the same person again.

Bon voyage.

WHY ARE SOME
PEOPLE SO SUCCESSFUL?

Have you ever wondered why some people are more successful than others? Why is it that some people enjoy better health, happier relationships, greater success in their careers, and achieve financial independence, if not great wealth—and others do not? What is it that enables some people to accomplish remarkable things and enjoy wonderful lives while so many others feel frustrated and disappointed?

These questions were important to me when I started out in life. I came from humble beginnings. My parents were good people, but they were not always regularly employed. Growing up, we never seemed to have enough money for anything. Our family theme song was, "We can't afford it!"

I didn't graduate from high school. I didn't quit or drop out, but I left high school in the half of the class that made the top half possible. At the commencement ceremony, instead of a diploma, I got a simple "Leaving Certificate."

My first full-time job was as a dishwasher in a small hotel. I started at 4 p.m. and often worked into the early hours of the morning. When I lost that job, I got a job washing cars on a car lot. When I lost that job, I got a job with a janitorial service washing floors late into the night. I began to think that washing things was going to be in my future.

With a limited education, I seemed to have a limited future as well. I worked in a sawmill stacking lumber on the afternoon shift and then later, the graveyard shift, getting off at 7 a.m. I pumped gas and worked at odd jobs. I worked in the bush with a chainsaw, on a logging crew, sometimes 12 hours a day, enduring black flies, dust, diesel fuel, and 90-degree heat. I even dug wells for a while. That's where you start at ground level and work up. And when you succeed, you fail, because when you find water, they fire you. It was not a great incentive system.

I was homeless before it was respectable. I lived in my car in the winter and slept next to it in the summer. I worked in hotels and restaurants, washing pots and pans in the winter and working on ranches and farms in the summer. I worked in construction as a laborer and in factories putting nuts on bolts, hour after hour.

I worked on a ship, a Norwegian freighter in the North Atlantic, as a galley boy, the lowest man on the nautical totem pole. I worked and drifted from odd job to odd job for years, continually asking and wondering, "Why are some people more successful than others?"

My life is different now. I live in a beautiful house on a golf course in Southern California. I have a beautiful family and successful business with operations throughout the United States, Canada, and in a dozen foreign countries. And all this because I finally found the answers.

After years of searching, I met a wise and wealthy man who sat me down and told me the key to success. He also explained the reasons for failure and under-achievement in life. As he spoke, I immediately recognized the truth in what he said. And his discovery about success was quite simple, as all great truths seem to be.

What he told me was this: **The key to success is for you to set one great, challenging goal and then to pay any price, overcome any obstacle and persist through any difficulty until you finally achieve it."**

By achieving one important goal, you create a pattern, a template for success in your subconscious mind. Ever after you will be automatically directed and driven toward repeating that success in other things that you attempt. By overcoming adversity and achieving one great objective, you will program yourself for success in life.

In other words, *you learn to succeed by succeeding. The more you achieve, the more you can achieve.*

You can accomplish almost any goal that you set for yourself if you persist long enough and work hard enough. The only one who can stop you is yourself. And you learn to persist by persisting in the face of great adversity when everyone around you is quitting and every fiber of your being screams at you to quit as well.

When you subject certain chemicals to intense heat, the chemicals will crystallize and form a completely new substance, a new composition in which the crystallization process is irreversible. A lump of coal becomes a diamond under intense prolonged heat and pressure. In the same way, you become a great person by persevering in the crucible of intense difficulty until you finally succeed. Each time you persevere, your character "crystallizes" at a new, higher level. Eventually, you reach the point where you become unstoppable.

It has been said that the ultimate aim of life is to become a person of character. A person of character is one in whom the great virtues of courage, persistence, compassion, generosity, integrity, tenacity, and perseverance have crystallized in such a way that they have created within you an unshakable set of principles that you will not compromise under any circumstances.

And it's not easy. Every extraordinary achievement in life is a result of thousands of ordinary efforts that no one ever sees or appreciates.

As the poet Longfellow once wrote:

> *Those heights by great men, won and kept,*
> *Were not achieved by sudden flight;*
> *But they, while their companions slept,*
> *Were toiling upwards in the night.*

When you complete a major task, overcome a great obstacle or achieve an important goal, you experience the emotions of exhilaration, joy, satisfaction, happiness, and personal pride. You set a pattern in your subconscious mind that forever after motivates you to repeat the same type of experience that leads to the same feelings.

You learn to be brave by being brave. You learn to persist by persisting. You learn to overcome by overcoming. The character you form and develop is in direct proportion to the height or intensity of these qualities demanded by the difficult situation, multiplied by the length of time that you demonstrate these qualities in the face of adversity.

Entrepreneurs and business people become successful as a direct result of trying and failing over and over again, and then picking themselves up and pressing on. Each time they refuse to be stopped by a setback or disappointment, they reinforce a pattern that enables them to persist more readily the next time.

Eventually, they reach a state of mind where they become unstoppable. Failure for them is not an option. They become irresistible forces of nature. They reach the point in their own minds where they cannot conceive of any outcome except final victory. And this must be your goal as well.

Here is some good news: *you have within you, right now, everything you could ever need or want to be a great success in any area of your life that you consider to be important.*

You have within you deep reserves of potential and ability that, properly harnessed and channeled, will enable you to accomplish extraordinary things with your life. The only real limits on what you can do, have, or be are self-imposed.

Once you make a clear, conscious decision to cast off all your mental limitations and throw your whole heart into the accomplishment of some great goal, you will ultimately succeed, as long as you don't stop.

But I am getting ahead of myself. We learn most of our great lessons in life by looking back at what happened to us, by evaluating those experiences and by extracting ideas and insights from them that we can then apply to the future.

The turning point in my life came many years ago, although I did not recognize it at the time. Afterwards, however, I felt that I could accomplish just about anything, if I wanted it badly enough and was willing to work long enough and hard enough. And this is true for you as well.

I spent many years traveling around the world, but the "crucible experience" of my life was my first big trip, my first great journey into the unknown. In a very positive way, I never recovered from it. The experiences that I had at that time and the lessons that I learned were burned into my brain and affected my outlook on life forever after. I have never been the same since the Sahara crossing.

THE STORY

This story is about a trip. It is a story for people who travel and enjoy it, and for people who want to travel but never seize the opportunity. Really, it is a story for anyone who sets out toward a distant goal and enjoys the steps to get there as much as the arrival. The more inclined you are to look upon life as a journey, and success as a journey, the more likely you will actually enjoy your life, and every step of the way.

My heartfelt desire is that you will not only understand this story about traveling but also feel, at least in part, like a member of the team, making progress from place to place, covering as much ground as possible, in order to achieve the goal.

Traveling, in its purest form—that is, separate from occupational, recreational, educational, and social excursions—has been described by the author John Steinbeck as the "urge to be someplace else," but there is more to it than that.

It is the desire to wake in the morning and see the mist on the road, knowing that the miles ahead will be brand new, consisting of people, places, and experiences completely unpredictable and unknowable. It is the feeling of detachment and freedom from the environment, while being at the same time so involved with it physically and emotionally that the body tingles with eagerness and anticipation. The overwhelming sensation of a true traveler is the joyous exhilaration that comes through motion, not once, but over and over again, creating a state of continual elation and, underneath, a contentment and peace bordering on paradise.

There are few true travelers, and of these, none are full time. Like malaria, the traveling "bug" enters the bloodstream, often through a tiny prick in the consciousness—a book, a song, a poem perhaps—and builds up in the body silently. Then one day the fever strikes with an intensity causing an incredible dissatisfaction with routine and normal living.

The cost of traveling is high. To be a true traveler means severing bonds, leaving behind friends, family and security, casting one's fate into the teeth of the unknown—and not many people dare to pay this price. Those who answer the "call of the road," and are mentally suited to it, are among the happiest people on earth, and do not need to die to know what heaven is.

Those who dare not leave their social obligations and security behind always carry with them the vague feeling that they have missed something important. Throughout their lives, they will be troubled by recurring periods of uneasiness that they can't explain to themselves, or to anyone else. And they need not die to have a taste of hell.

The traveling life, though costly, is so enriching emotionally and mentally that it does not, and cannot, last for long periods. It usually leaves the traveler spent and fulfilled, quite prepared to accept the regularity of a quiet life in exchange for the joyous uncertainty of the road.

The traveling life is essentially an individual one, best embarked upon alone, or with a close companion, with whom one is in complete accord—and this is asking a lot.

Any true traveler reading this account understands clearly what I'm trying to say. I was a young man when I came to these conclusions, but years of practical experience have only reconfirmed their essential truth.

If you feel the call, "the lure of little voices, all abegging you to go," don't fight it and don't be afraid of it. Take hold of it with both hands and kick yourself free. Live it until you know yourself—and then go back, if you can. It's not an easy life, even if you do it right; it can be deadly difficult if you do it wrong. But, if you're meant for it, it's surely the greatest life on earth.

My friends Geoff, Bob, and I left home seeking changes and challenges, to be endured at the time and bragged about later. When viewed by romantic souls, these hard times become glorious "adventures." Over the miles, we learned a lot about traveling, a lot about Europe and Africa, a lot about living, and a lot about life. Each lesson was learned through physical experience, and each benefit gained through practical application.

We grew up as normal children, in that we each thought of ourselves as rather extraordinary young men with high moral ideals and romantic ideas about how people should behave and how things should be done, on the basis of what we'd read and been taught. For example, we considered reminders like, "Be strong," "Be brave," and "Keep smiling" to be fine and noble, applicable to any difficulty; that is, until we found ourselves sitting in the Sahara by an empty road in 120 degrees of bake-oven heat, with 2,000 miles between us and our destination. Just about then, we began to wonder about the merits of noble ideals. And the situation had not the slightest resemblance to an adventure.

Out of this and countless other experiences, others a good deal worse, came a gradual realization that *a large gulf exists between the Pollyanna platitudes and reality.*

THREE WAYS TO READ THIS BOOK

I suggest that there are three ways this book can be read. The first is to read the book *as a travel adventure.* In writing this narrative, spanning two years of the most impressionable time of my life, I have tried to be purely objective, relying on our many unusual experiences to make the story worthwhile reading—assuming that a vivid account of three young men who set a goal 17,000 miles away, and then went about getting there, would be sufficiently interesting to justify the writing of it.

However, I also have laced the narrative with bits of philosophy. And, as I neared the completion of this story, I discovered truths so universal that they can be removed entirely from the context, to stand alone as lessons applicable to any situation. So, this tale of traveling to and through Africa assumes an added dimension.

Second, the story can be read *as an account of a search for truth.* The beginning is innocence, marked by questions and curiosity. When the search begins in earnest, many obstacles arise, most notably that of ignorance—of how to pursue the quest. The search crosses barren terrain and several borders, and covers times when knowledge and experience are concentrated into short bursts of enlightenment.

There is confusion and dishonesty. There are dangers and hardships. There is the necessity for perseverance and ingenuity. There is the need for assistance from other people and the realization that no one does it alone.

When the truth comes, it is overwhelming and requires a violent rearrangement of previous beliefs, leaving us a bit older and wiser, and perhaps with an understanding of what it means to suffer.

The third way this story can be read is *as a biography of a person* going through a complete metamorphosis. There is the conception, the prenatal preparations, and then the birth. There is a childhood, a troubled one, and long. There is an adolescence, confused and uncertain, a young maturity, and a striving middle age, complete with disillusion and resolute plodding along a straight line. At last comes old age, and in this instance, an empty, exhausted arrival at the "other side."

Whichever way you look at it—as a story about traveling, as a search for truth, or as a biography—one thing is clear: It is entirely true. And as we saw it, it was absolutely necessary. Geoff, Bob, and I did it, as many others have and will, and it doesn't matter who you are—sooner or later, *everyone has a Sahara to cross.*

SECTION 1:
THE VISION AND DREAM

Every great achievement begins with a vision, a dream of something exciting or different, a feeling that inspires and motivates you to aim higher than you ever have before.

What is your vision for your life? Imagine for a moment that you have no limitations on what you can be or do. Imagine that you have all the time and all the money, all the knowledge and experience, all the skills and resources, all the friends and contacts. If you could have anything in your life, what would it be?

Project forward five years and imagine that your life is *now* perfect in every way. What does it look like? What are you doing? Who is there with you? Who is no longer there? Describe your perfect future.

Allow yourself to "dream big dreams." Decide what's right before you decide what's possible. Imagine your future as ideal in every respect, and remember: Whatever others have done, you can probably do as well.

Once you've decided where you're going, the only question to ask is "How?" How do you get from where you are today to where you want to be? And remember, failure is not an option.

CHAPTER 1

THE CALL OF THE OPEN ROAD

Some people are born to stay at home. Others are born to travel. I suppose the things we dream about and plan toward are good indications of our preferences.

When Geoff and I were 16, we were already talking about how quickly we would be on the road when our schooling was finished. One day I found a poem in the school library and ever after let it speak our aims and ambitions, and the attitude we would adopt toward our lives, and later, our traveling. Perhaps we already felt this way, but no one had ever summed it up quite as well as Robert W. Service in "The Lone Trail":

> The trails of the world be countless, and most of the trails
>   be tried;
> You tread on the heels of the many, till you come where the
>   ways divide;
> And one lies safe in the sunlight, and the other is dreary
>   and wan,
> But you look aslant at the Lone Trail, and the Lone Trail
>   lures you on.

That was the general idea. The doing of something different, not necessarily for the sake of being different, but because we thought the best way to express our individuality, and the only way we could enjoy life, was to refuse to be satisfied with the commonplace. But to do that you have to pay a price, of sorts, as the poem goes on to say:

> Bid good-bye to sweetheart, bid good-bye to friend,
> The Lone Trail, the Lone Trail follow to the end.
> Tarry not and fear not, chosen of the true;
> Lover of the Lone Trail, the Lone Trail waits for you.

Of course, at 16, we really didn't know what the poet was talking about, but it sounded good, and whatever he meant, we agreed with it wholeheartedly.

The call first sounded for us when we were 17, drawing us to the north woods for the summer to fight fires on various forestry crews. When we were 18, the call came from Southern California and Mexico with a craving to taste Tequila and see Hollywood. Within a year after leaving high school, we had worn out two cars each in the high country around Vancouver, and back into British Columbia. In summer 1963, the call came from the east, luring us over the Rocky Mountains to the prairies and beyond.

That fall, Geoff went to a university, completing his second semester in May 1964. I was working the graveyard shift at a local sawmill at that time, quite contentedly, when he came by my apartment one morning and woke me up. He had come to say good-bye.

"Where are you going?" I asked sleepily.

"To Winnipeg," he replied. "I'm going to work there for the summer."

"Yeah, when are you going to settle down and start becoming a respectable citizen?"

"Next year, for sure."

"Well, you can start being a good citizen right now by letting me go back to sleep. When are you leaving?"

"Now."

"What?!"

"Right now. I'm on my way out of town."

"Humph! You'd better write when you get an address. I might join you later this summer."

"I'll be expecting you. So long."

With a heigh-ho and a happy wave, he puttered out of the parking lot in his battered Pontiac and turned onto Georgia Street, heading for the trans-Canada highway leading eastward.

It was the end of July before I caught up with him, rolling into Winnipeg after a sweep through British Columbia and Northern Alberta, coming down through Saskatchewan to Regina, and then into Manitoba and the queen city of the province. Winnipeg was 1,600 miles from Vancouver and represented the farthest we'd been from home.

I found Geoff working a construction job at the airport. That night we decided that since we had already come this far, we might as well see Toronto, 1,600 miles farther, before we settled down. A week later, in response to a telegram, Tom Culbert, our best friend from Vancouver, hitchhiked out to join us. Geoff quit his job. We pooled our finances, loaded our few clothes into my 1951 Chevy, and we were on our way.

We had mapped out a route that would take us south and east under the Great Lakes via Chicago and up to Detroit, over the border and on to Toronto, then back. However, we became infected with the enchanting lure of the open road.

"We might never get another chance," we told ourselves, and our route and destination began changing every day or two. We found that we could get by on one meal a day, and that was all we ate for the rest of the trip.

In the next month we went through Minneapolis, Chicago, Cincinnati, and down into the southern United States to Miami, Florida, coming up the Atlantic seaboard through Philadelphia, Washington, D.C., New York, Montreal, Toronto, and then finally over the Great Lakes and back to Winnipeg.

Four weeks later, after a total of 17 states, six provinces, and 12,000 miles, we wearily arrived back in Vancouver, thoroughly glutted with faraway places and more than ready to settle down.

I had worked for the first year after leaving school and had concluded that higher education was something much to be desired if I didn't want to sweat for a living for the rest of my days. I enrolled in a series of courses a week later and got a job on the night shift of a sawmill to earn the funds I had neglected to set aside in the previous year. Geoff found a similar job in a plywood mill and decided to concentrate on working for a year, planning to return to his education the following fall.

We had traveled on a starvation budget, sleeping in the old Chevy when it rained, in parks and fields when it didn't, eating very little in order to save what money we had for gasoline. Often we drove for two or three days at a stretch, living on cigarettes and nervous energy, and we mistook the fatigue resulting from a month of this to be satiation with travel. The thought of giving up a life with a definite purpose and a future, to do it again, was out of the question. However, we made one concession.

On Thanksgiving weekend in October 1964, when we had three days free of school and work, we packed the Chevy and drove 1,100 miles south to see San Francisco. It took 22 hours of steady motoring to get there, and after a rollicking, happy day and a half, it took 22 hours to get back. And we finally gave up fooling ourselves.

We were hooked on traveling. The complacency that had marked our attitude after our return from the east had turned sour. We spoke about it often and decided that we had exhausted North America as a place to tour. We had loved every minute of it, but now we wanted to see something different, something unusual, something with more challenge. But where?

The obvious answer was Europe, the old world, the land of our forefathers. But everyone who traveled went to Europe. Many of our friends had already been and returned, and many others were preparing to go. We wanted to do something different.

No, Europe was not the answer. Later perhaps, but not the first time we set foot off the North American continent. We discussed variations and alternatives for a long time, before we finally decided on Africa!

It filled all the requirements. Just to think of it—the dark continent. Black Africa, pygmies, Zulus, lions, elephants, savagery, splendor, tribal dances, exotic jungles, and adventure. Our imaginations leaped and tumbled with a thousand different images and fantasies.

Of course, it never occurred to us to ask why it was that no one else was going to Africa. That was our first mistake. We would find that out ourselves at great price in the fullness of time.

I later learned that *all great ventures entail great risks, the willingness to "go boldly where no one has ever gone before."*

There seemed little point in discussing our decision with anyone. We had learned from past experience that nothing kills an idea so completely as endless discussion, idle chatter, and empty speculation. Besides, no one among our acquaintances knew anything about Africa and so we kept our plan to ourselves. In the weeks to follow, without more than an occasional chat on a possible route, the thought of Africa became the focal point of our lives. This ambition stood as an exciting pillar of assurance. No matter how bored or disgruntled we became, we could always look inward and chuckle, "It won't be for much longer; we'll soon be on our way to Africa."

WHAT IS YOUR PERSONAL MISSION?

You have been put on this earth to do some great thing with your life, to do something wonderful that will benefit both yourself and others.

You have within you enormous untapped resources of talent and ability—just waiting to be harnessed and challenged toward some great good.

Be honest with yourself. Don't fall into the trap of selling yourself short, of accepting less than you're truly capable of. You were born for greatness. You are here to make a difference with your life in some way.

What do you really want? If you could be or do or have anything in life, what would it be? Allow yourself to dream, and then go to work to make your dreams come true.

"Have you built your castles in the air? Good! That's where they should be built. Now, go to work and build foundations under them."—**Henry David Thoreau**

CHAPTER 2

THE PREPARATION

Because of my school and the need to put aside money, we set a tentative departure date for late August 1965. Early in the year, Geoff's sister, Pamela, announced her engagement and intention to marry on September 19. We then decided to attend the wedding and leave September 20. That would give us ample time to pay off an accumulation of small debts and build a healthy bank account.

In April 1965, we brought Bob MacDonald, our good friend, into the planning. Up to that point, we had largely contented ourselves with glorious fantasies and romantic speculation. Bob was a big, robust fellow with an easy laugh and an outgoing personality with whom we played football and drank beer on the weekends. He wanted naturally to know what we had done toward preparing for our departure. It dawned on us that we had not done much beyond talking about it during the last three months. It was time we got down to business.

Our preparations went from fanciful chat to serious steps toward the great adventure. We formed a club, the Bon Vivants, and made the dark continent our first project. We began writing to every travel bureau whose address we could unearth. In the ensuing months we received a prodigious mass of information from all over the world, but unfortunately it was largely composed of brochures on luxury hotels, expensive cruises, guided tours, all-inclusive safaris, and jet and ocean liner fares—all far beyond our humble means. There were, however, some useful bits of information, and these we gleaned and set aside for future reference.

We began a series of inoculations to withstand the assaults of smallpox, tetanus, yellow fever, cholera, typhus, poliomyelitis, and blackwater fever. After three months of regular visits to the health center, we felt confident that we would never contract another disease. We even took an Industrial First Aid course to be prepared in case of an accident.

To finance the trip, we opened a bank account and started depositing $5 per week each. In April we increased the sum to $10 and subsequently raised the amount $5 a month for the rest of the time we were in North Vancouver. For the three weeks before departure in September, the ante was $35, bringing the account to almost

$2,000. It seemed like a lot, but once underway, the money didn't last very long.

I learned later in life that *everything ends up costing about twice as much as you thought and taking three times longer.* These forecasts are especially true in starting any new business or introducing any new product or service. They certainly proved true for traveling.

During July and August, the Bon Vivants rented a furnished five-bedroom house in the neighborhood where we'd grown up and gone to school. It became the social center of our group. By mid-July, 11 of us were living there. In late August, we invited all our friends to a going-away party.

Over 200 people came, and the band played until the early hours of the morning. The whole house shook with music and laughter. The sun was high in the sky before the last guests departed.

The restoration of the house to its original condition, better in fact, took a week of hard work and cost over $200. It was cheap at twice the price. Our adult lives had begun.

THE MASTERSKILL OF SUCCESS

Your ability to set goals and make plans for their accomplishment is the "masterskill" of success.

The 10/90 rule says that, "The first 10 percent of time you spend planning and organizing will often account for 90 percent of the value of the entire process."

Here is a powerful but simple method for setting and achieving goals:

1. Decide exactly what you want. Clarity is the starting point of great success.

2. Write it down, in detail, and set a deadline. Set sub-deadlines if necessary.

3. Determine the additional knowledge, skills, and abilities you will need to achieve your goal—and how you will acquire them.

4. Determine the obstacles and difficulties you will have to overcome and organize them in order of size and importance.

5. Determine the people, groups, and organizations whose assistance you will require, and decide what you will have to do to earn their help.

6. Make a detailed plan, broken down by activity and organized based on priority and importance. What do you do first? What is more important? What is less important?

7. Take action on your plan immediately. Do something every day to move toward your goal. Develop momentum and keep it up.

SECTION 2:
STARTING OUT—JUST DO IT!

"A journey of a thousand leagues begins with a single step," wrote Confucius. A thousand dreams die unborn every day because the dreamer lacks the courage to take the first step, in faith, with no guarantees of success.

The great difference between high achievement and failure in life is contained in your willingness to launch in the direction of your goal, even when your information is still incomplete.

There are no guarantees in life, and we know that if every question must be answered, if every obstacle must first be overcome—then nothing will ever get done.

Decide what you want, write it down, make a plan, and then—take action.

"Leap and the net will appear!"

CHAPTER 3

THE FIRST STEP: VANCOUVER TO MONTREAL, CANADA

On a Sunday evening at 10 p.m., three weeks later, in a cold drizzling rain, we bid our families and friends our last good-byes, severing the final ties with our youth and 20 years of life. I turned the old 1948 Chevy eastward, and we left Vancouver behind us in the night. It was September 20, 1965.

I learned later that *every successful enterprise, great or small, begins with a leap of faith, a driving into the dark, into the unknown.* Nature is kind to us in that she never lets us see too far ahead. *If we really knew all the difficulties, disappointments, temporary failures, and heartaches we would experience, most of us would not start out at all.* This applies to new businesses, careers, marriage, having children—and almost every other human endeavor.

That was the beginning. It was rather anticlimatic after a year of planning and looking forward to the big moment. For a long time, we were understandably silent, each wrapped up in his own thoughts as we drove into the night. We were off to see the world.

We drove all night, stopping for gas or coffee occasionally (the Chevy burned a quart of oil every 50 miles), but more or less driving steadily north, then east across the Rocky Mountains. The magnificent unspoiled beauty of Rodgers Pass was behind us the next morning when the sun rose through the clouds over Banff, Alberta, where we stopped for breakfast. We arrived in Calgary early in the afternoon and checked into the YMCA for the night.

On our way across the country, we stopped in Regina and stayed with friends for two days. We checked into a motel in Winnipeg for two more nights, then turned south into the States toward the Great Lakes. The weather was bad—nothing but howling winds and icy rains most of the way.

The tank-like Chevy that we had bought for the trip was riding very low on its springs and using an alarming quantity of gas and oil, but by and large, the car held together quite well. We only had one emergency, and that was on our way to Chicago through Iowa. The brakes failed altogether.

This problem was first discovered by Bob as we drove about 50 miles an hour in the rain, late at night, and on a curve. He yelped, "The brakes are gone!"

"Pump them up! Pump them up" we shouted.

"I've been pumping them for the last hour! There's nothing left to pump!"

He geared down to second and shut off the engine, bringing the car to a jerky halt a quarter of a mile later. The brake cylinder was dry, and we were 85 miles from the next large town. The highway was dark and empty, and the cold wind howled across the silent cornfields on both sides.

Since there was no traffic on the road, we decided to drive the car slowly until we found an open service station where we could buy some brake fluid. It was 11:30 at night when I got behind the wheel.

It seemed like the entire state was asleep. Town after quiet town slipped past the rain-spattered Chevy as we crept along, peering down the darkened side streets looking for the lights of a service station. About two hours later, we came to the outskirts of Dubuque, a large town with considerable traffic, even at that hour.

After helplessly coasting through two red lights with no garage in sight, we became more cautious, driving in first gear, approaching intersections as furtively as thieves.

Then, coming down a slight grade, we arrived at a busy cross street. A steady stream of traffic passed ahead of us, and a red light faced us. The Chevy was already in first gear with the engine cut, but we could see we wouldn't stop in time to avoid coasting right into the traffic.

At just about the same moment, we all had the same idea and leaped out of the car and into the street. Throwing every bit of weight we could muster, feet skidding along the wet pavement, we soon brought the beast to a halt. Six feet in front of us, an express bus roared through the intersection, whipping us with a windy spray. Laughing delightedly at our newfound brakes, we congratulated each other and climbed back inside.

Twice more this course of action became necessary before we found an all-night service station and refilled the thirsty brake cylinder. From the looks on the faces of passing motorists, we deduced that this sort of thing wasn't done too often in Dubuque, Iowa. We had no further difficulties with the vehicle after that.

For the next two days we drove steadily, not stopping to sleep at all. After half a day in Chicago, we drove out and followed Lake Michigan through Gary, Indiana, and on up the expressway to Detroit. There we crossed back into Canada, continuing through

Windsor to Toronto, and another night at the YMCA. The following evening, we rumbled into Montreal, 3,200 miles from Vancouver, and the end of the first leg of our long trip to Africa.

Before starting this adventure, we had made several excursions without sleeping, driving non-stop to save time. Sometimes we traded off when one of us began falling asleep. This experience, to which we gave little thought at the time, of driving for two or three days without sleep, even when we were so tired we began to hallucinate, would serve us well in the months ahead. It may have saved our lives.

We had made Montreal our first objective, to be accomplished within 10 days and with a minimum of expense. It took us nine days and cost just $200 for everything, including gasoline and oil (and brake fluid!), food, motels and YMCAs, and beer. The weather was bad but our spirits were high, and we rolled into Montreal singing, all four of us in the front seat. It was a grand beginning.

From Montreal, our next objective was London, England—the cheapest way possible. For three days, we tramped the waterfront seeking a Europe-bound ship needing crew members. However, with winter in the air, there were few ships in the inland port, and they had no vacancies for unskilled seamen. It soon became obvious that we weren't going to get a job that would save us the cost of the fare.

After discussing it for awhile, we agreed that not only was it too late in the year to find a job on a boat, but also it was too late to start for Africa, even if we did manage to get to Europe. We decided to work somewhere for the winter and set off in the spring. The question was, where?

THE ADVENTURE BEGINS

For you to accomplish any great good, you will have to learn certain lessons and gain new knowledge and experience. From the moment you actually launch a new venture, you will begin to learn at an accelerated rate.

As it happens, we only learn when it costs us money or emotion, or both. There seems to be no other way.

The key is for you to look to any setback or obstacle for the valuable lesson or benefit that it contains. Focus on the future; forget the past. Think about the solution rather than the problem.

Keep asking, "What's the solution? What is this situation meant to teach us? What do we do now?"

CHAPTER 4

THE FIRST CRISIS

This situation in Montreal triggered the first crisis on our trip. One of the guys decided to quit and hitchhike home. The other two, Geoff and Bob, decided to stop looking for a job on a ship and use their limited funds instead to purchase passage on a freighter headed for England.

I was appalled. I tried to talk them out of it. I told them that *quitting is a habit.* If they quit now, the first time we met resistance and disappointment, they would always quit. They would establish a pattern for failure rather than a pattern for success. It was a matter of principle.

But their minds were made up. So we split our savings, and they used half of their money to book passage on a ship. I decided that it was too late in the year to go to Africa anyway and resolved to stay in Montreal for the winter. Our partnership was officially dissolved, just two weeks after starting out.

I later learned that *partnerships are the worst of all forms of business relationships.* They start off with high hopes and usually end with dashed expectations, ruined friendships, and mutual recriminations.

I got a job as a construction laborer, carrying heavy things from place to place, and later as a factory worker, screwing nuts onto bolts hour after hour. I rented a tiny one-room apartment with a foldout bed and a small kitchen. The temperature that winter fell to 35 degrees below zero, and life seemed very bleak indeed.

Here I was, 20 years old, 3,200 miles from my family, with no intention of going back home. I had failed high school, fooling around and working as a dishwasher in a small hotel rather than studying. I was uneducated, unskilled, and regularly unemployed. And I wanted to go to Africa.

I still remember that fateful night, sitting at my little kitchen table, alone, with the cold winter wind howling outside. It suddenly dawned on me that *everything and anything I ever accomplished in life was up to me. I was completely responsible. No one was ever going to do it for me.* If I did not take charge of my life, nothing was ever going to change. I would remain an underpaid laborer, pinching pennies and worrying about money for the rest of my life.

SUCCESS IS A JOURNEY

It was an incredible revelation! I determined right there and then that my future would be different from my past. I wrote out a series of goals for myself and resolved to take action on them. That night, that realization, was the turning point in my life.

The next day, I began to study French, preparing for my travels in France and Africa. I took karate lessons three times per week. I began reading every book I could get on every subject that interested me. I became a lifelong student of personal development and personal success.

At the end of February, I packed all my belongings in an old trunk and shipped them to Halifax, the biggest port on the Atlantic coast. I then hitchhiked my way there and checked into the local YMCA.

My goal was to get a job on a ship, work my way to England, join my friends again and proceed toward Africa. I got up early that cold winter morning and began scouring the waterfront, visiting every ship at the docks and asking if they needed a crewman to England.

By the end of the day, I had gone to every ship on the waterfront and had been turned down every time. Tired and defeated, I made my way up the long hill back to the warmth of the YMCA, wondering what I would do now.

Just as I reached the front door of the YMCA, I looked back toward the waterfront and saw two ships loading at a dock somewhat apart from the other ships. I hadn't seen them before. I looked longingly at the warmth and comfort of the YMCA but then forced myself to trudge down the long hill to the ships and give it one more try.

The first ship was going down the east coast of the U.S., but the second ship, the Norwegian freighter Nordpohl, was going to Manchester, England, and yes, they had an opening for a galley boy for the crossing. The job was mine, if I could be on board and ready to depart by 8 p.m. that night, just two hours away!

I was ecstatic! I had a job. My last shot had paid off. My goal, my dream of working my way across the Atlantic on a ship, was realized. Could I be ready to depart in two hours? You bet!

One great lesson I learned from this experience, and again and again later in life, was that *your greatest success, your great breakthrough, often comes one step beyond where you are ready to quit, to throw in the towel.* It is almost as though nature places a final "persistence test" in your path just to test you, to see how badly you really want it. As the poem says:

And you never can tell how close you are,
It may be near when it seems so far.
So stick to the fight when you're hardest hit,
It's when things seem worst that you must not quit.

At 8 p.m. I was on board as the ship cast its lines and headed out into the Atlantic. I stood on the bow of the ship as the city of Halifax disappeared into the night. I was really off to see the world!

IT'S TESTING TIME!

Life is a continuous succession of problems, large and small. They never stop. The only thing about problems you can change is your response to them, positive or negative, helpful or hurtful.

Most people quit at the first crisis. They collapse, like tents with the center poles removed. They give up and retreat to their comfort zones, at lower levels of challenge and accomplishment.

But this is not for you! Your job is to view every crisis as a "test," to teach you something you need to know to be more successful in the future.

Resolve in advance that no matter what happens, you will never give up. You will bounce rather than break. You will keep on keeping on until you succeed.

CHAPTER 5

STARTING AGAIN

At the end of March 1966, I signed off the Norwegian freighter Nordpohl, in Manchester, and took a train up to Coventry in the English Midlands to join Geoff and Bob. It had been a long, cold winter on the construction crew after we decided to go separate ways until the spring. They had taken a ship to Amsterdam in the first week of October. They had arrived in England four weeks later and then gone to Coventry to visit friends of Geoff's family, staying through the winter working as lifeguards at the public baths in that city.

Before settling in for the winter, they had set off for Africa by themselves, taking the ferry from Dover to Calais and trying to hitchhike across France. But French drivers don't stop for hitchhikers. After many hours of waiting by the side of the road, just as I had predicted some months ago in Montreal, they quit again. They then made their way back to England for the winter. They didn't know, as most people don't, that *quitting is an insidious habit that grows so slowly one is unaware of its enticements until it is so deeply ingrained that it cuts off all hope of success and great achievement.*

Now spring was in the air. The country was lovely and green, as the travel posters show, and early flowers brightened the tiny thatched villages along the course of the railway. There was a magic sparkle in the air that one could feel dancing along the skin, bringing with it a restlessness and an urge to be out doing things. As the train rumbled across the English countryside toward Coventry, I was thinking how strange it was that we would plan and anticipate for over a year, and then be dormant for six months.

I suppose it was the launch that had been the important thing, that first step, that cutting loose and casting off, leaving the familiar ways far behind. All around us in Vancouver, friends and acquaintances from school and work were getting married and settling into careers. A pattern of day-to-day living was forming; the grip of adulthood and maturity was tightening.

But we had broken the pattern, like colts shaking off the traces and running free, kicking up our heels, secure in knowing that when we tired of the open pasture we could always return to the security and stability of the lives we had put behind us. So it did not matter if we stopped somewhere for the winter; we were free, unfettered by responsibility and the necessity to account for our present and future. Surely in a year or two we would have to return, like prodigal sons, and earn our places in the well-ordered society. But we couldn't be satisfied with one place until we'd grown tired of looking at the others, and that wouldn't be for a long time.

I learned later that *the most important thing is to launch, to begin with no guarantee of success.* Once you start, everything changes. New avenues and opportunities open up for you—openings that you could not have seen had you not been in forward motion. "Leap and the net will appear!"

The taxi dropped me at the Stoke Hill Guildhouse late that afternoon. I soon found the narrow, cement-floored room of my two friends. It was locked, and since they were not to be found on the grounds among the other working people coming from jobs in the mills and factories of Coventry, I climbed in the window and made myself comfortable. As the sun went down, I drifted off to sleep peacefully. It had been a long trip.

Three hours later, they came in singing, startling me awake with their drunken rendition of "She loves you, yeah, yeah, yeah." Bob was halfway into bed when he saw me sitting there, blinking at the sudden light and noise. His face broke into a mile-wide grin, and we clasped hands with a joyous whoop. Geoff was right behind him, and for five minutes we laughed, asked questions, and tried to catch up on five months in one bubbling outburst. It was like old home week.

After we'd quieted down a bit, I began telling of my life at sea, and the bully on the ship that had turned out not to be so tough after all. Bob got out his suitcase and showed me the picture of himself from the newspaper, after he had won the third-place ribbon in the "Mr. Coventry" bodybuilding contest that January. Suddenly there came a harsh rap on the door.

It was a pair of English bobbies investigating a report that an Austin van had knocked through a barrier in a nearby automatic parking lot. The license number was suspiciously identical to that of the van driven by Geoff and Bob. They hadn't had a shilling for the automatic gate release and in their inebriated state had said, "What the hell?" and driven right through it. After long arguments, denials, and promises to pay in the morning, the police departed, and we all had a good laugh.

The planning and discussion were wisely put off until the morning when clearer heads would prevail.

Once again we were on our way to Africa. The boys had a lot of good-byes to say after five months in Coventry, and we had a lot of beers together to catch up on. But three days later, everything was wrapped up, the van was sold, and we caught the morning train for London. Most of our luggage, including the big trunk I had brought from Montreal, was sent to Potter's Bar, a hamlet north of London, where we hoped to leave it with my aunt.

Russell Square, an area known for its inexpensive bed and breakfast hotels, was a 20-minute walk from Euston Station, where we arrived at noon. Taking turns lugging the two over-stuffed suitcases, we inquired until we found a hotel with a vacancy for three and a landlady with some imagination with regard to price. After a little haggling, she agreed to give us a reduction if one of us would sleep on the floor in the room with one double bed. That was no hardship for three stout lads on their way to Africa.

REEVALUATING AND REGROUPING

Your ability to think, to apply your mind to your situation, is the greatest power you have.

When the situation around you is constantly changing and your knowledge is incomplete, the more often you stop the clock to assess your situation, the better decisions you will make.

Keep asking, "What are my assumptions? How could I test them? What changes will I have to make if my assumptions are wrong?"

Focus on what's right rather than who's right. The person who discovers he or she is on the wrong road fast, and turns back, is the one who makes the most progress.

CHAPTER 6

GETTING DOWN TO BUSINESS

We had left the actual planning of a route and mode of transportation to and through Africa until we were a little closer to the objective. One lesson in our previous traveling had repeated itself time and time again: *Be clear about the goal, but be flexible about the process of achieving it.* Sure, you must set reasonable goals as ultimate aims, and work toward achieving those goals, but the intermediate steps must not be predetermined too closely. *Each step toward an objective modifies and influences, to a greater or lesser degree, the following steps.* The greater the number of unknowns, the more flexibility you need to deal with the eventualities that arise. In our situation, since we were almost totally ignorant of the road ahead, we avoided making specific plans.

I learned later in life that *your willingness to continually re-evaluate your plans, especially when you experience stress or resistance, can be critical to your long-term success.* The willingness to question your best-laid plans, to consider the possibility that you could be wrong or misinformed, is the mark of a superior mind.

This attitude of accepting change and adapting to difficulties gave us a certain resilience and buoyancy that made it almost impossible for us to become downhearted or discouraged at the unexpected twists and turns of fate.

Our first objective had been to leave Vancouver with as much money as possible. The second had been to cross Canada to Montreal, spending as little money as possible. The third objective had been to reach London with a minimum of expense. Our fourth objective was to reach the crown colony of Gibraltar, on the very doorstep of the African continent. There we would decide on our fifth objective.

Sitting down in a small tea shop with an atlas containing a one-page map of Africa, including Europe, we worked out a tentative route. We would cross France and Spain to Gibraltar, sail across the straits to Morocco, cross the Atlas Mountains into the Sahara, and cross the desert to Senegal. From there we would follow the hump of Africa around and into Lagos, Nigeria, the modern capital of British influence in West Africa. Once in Lagos, we could decide whether to head directly south or cross through central Africa and then south through Kenya and Tanzania.

We knew that the decision would be dictated by conditions beyond our control, but we had no idea just how extensive would be the difference between what we had innocently planned and the reality.

We made the dreadful error of superimposing our experiences in North America onto our travel plans in Africa. We assumed that roads were roads and that we could travel from anywhere to anywhere without hindrance. I later learned that *unexamined assumptions lie at the root of most problems in life.*

Our route planned, we then discussed what mode of conveyance we would use. There were several methods available. Bob found that the cheapest way to travel from London to Johannesburg was by plane—it would cost just $300 each, which was all we had. We considered flying to South Africa and returning to Europe via Cairo, but disregarded the idea as being too expensive. We also rejected the idea of going by boat for the same reason. We decided to travel from London to Johannesburg by land—all the way.

Since our map clearly showed roads through Africa, it was evident that many people had already driven through the continent. We reasoned, falsely, that there couldn't be much challenge in following the footsteps of countless others, and besides, a vehicle would be too expensive. We wanted to make the trip in a way that would bring us some glory. It would also have to be relatively inexpensive. What about bicycles?

Bicycles were cheap to buy, repair, and operate. We would understand the countries we passed through because of our limited speed and the necessity of living off the land. We would become physically hardened by pedaling all day and sleeping out each night. And we'd never heard of anyone making such a trip on a bicycle. There was no way of telling how much acclaim we could receive. We might even set a record or win a prize. Unanimously we agreed that bicycles were the answer.

That decided, there were two places we could buy bicycles. There in London, or in Gibraltar, after hitchhiking across France and Spain. The main argument for Gibraltar was that Africa was our objective, and we should get there with a minimum of delay. But with our limited knowledge, we decided to become accustomed to travelling on bicycles in the civilized countries of France and Spain. So, we set out to buy bicycles in London that very day.

This was another decision that probably saved us from our own innocence and ignorance. Just as in starting a business, *boot-strapping your way up on your profits from sales is usually better than starting with too much money. By starting with limited means, you are forced to fall back on your wits when you experience the inevitable disappointments that accompany any attempt to do anything new or different. As a result, you quickly develop the resilience and ingenuity that you must have to succeed later.*

When we arrived in London, our finances totaled just $1,000. From the start, we pooled the entire amount into what we dubbed the "company." Every purchase and expense were paid out of this cash pool. Having a common objective, we subordinated personal desires and pettiness to the common good. We agreed to be, "One for all, and all for one!"

Anything we bought or did was agreed upon unanimously. Anything any of us had, we all had, right down to underwear and razor blades. We would have many heated discussions and disagreements, but personal ownership never entered into them. After a while we no longer talked in terms of "I" and "me," but rather "we" and "the Bon Vivants."

We bought three used bicycles, three rucksacks, a kettle, a tiny stove, a frying pan, some cutlery, a few dishes, and a little brown teapot. From our belongings, we chose a few clothes that fit us all; a pair each of tennis shoes and jeans, socks, T-shirts, underwear, and three warm sweaters. A shaving kit, three towels, three books, and a radio completed the outfitting. Dressed in woolen caps and high-collared plastic rain jackets, we felt well attired for our crossing of Europe. And so, dividing the load evenly, we tied it onto our bicycles and pedaled out of London towards Potter's Bar.

At the time, Geoff was 20 years old and weighed a solid 180 pounds. Bob was a little taller and a little heavier, also solid at 184 pounds, spread over his rawboned frame. I was 21 and weighed 185 pounds, the heaviest and the oldest. I should have known better than to choose bicycles. But in those days, we were hopelessly optimistic.

We were bursting with energy and eagerness, bloated with ambition and high ideals; strong and happy and joyous at being at last on our way to Africa, the ultimate in high adventure. In those first carefree days, there was nowhere we couldn't go and nothing we couldn't do. We were indomitable, supermen, world-beaters on our way to Africa.

We had sent the things we couldn't take with us to the rail depot in Potter's Bar where my Aunt Barbara lived. We were hoping that she would have a place for us to store the things and perhaps somewhere we could sleep the night. We were in luck on both accounts. Although she was unsure at first which of us three strapping lads was her nephew, she not having seen me since I was 13, she readily threw open her little garage to us and offered a place to sleep the night. After bringing the trunk and the suitcases from the depot and storing them away, we sat down to explain our plans and intentions to "conquer Africa." Although we were tired from our 20-mile ride from London, we talked until midnight before going to bed in her little guest room.

Promising faithfully to return no later than October for a longer visit, we waved good-bye the next morning and rode toward Dover and France.

FLEXIBILITY IS THE KEY

The most important quality you can develop to assure great success in times of change and turbulence is the quality of flexibility.

Be open to new information. Be willing to accept feedback and self-correct. Be willing to admit that you could be wrong, that there could be a better way.

A famous military axiom says, "No strategy survives first contact with the enemy."

No plan, no matter how detailed, survives first contact with reality. Your job is to be clear about your goal, and flexible about the process of attaining it.

Section 3:
The Real Journey Begins at Last

Shakespeare wrote, "What's past is merely prelude." One of Murphy's Laws is, "Before you do anything, you have to do something else first." What we know for sure, at each stage of our lives, is that what's coming is more important than what has gone before.

Laurence Durrell, the author, once wrote, "I do not write for people who have never asked themselves, 'When does real life begin?'"

This life is not a rehearsal for something else. Successful, happy people live intensely in the moment, in the "now" of life and reality. They have learned to combine a long-term vision with a short-term focus. They are dreamers with their feet firmly planted in the reality of the current situation.

To achieve something you've never achieved before, you must become someone you've never been before. As Goethe said, "To have more, we must first become more."

The great majority of people want their success and happiness on the cheap, without paying full price for it, in advance, as nature demands. This continual striving after something for nothing, of achievement without expense, leads to frustration, failure, and impoverishment of spirit.

The good news is that nature is exceedingly generous. If you are willing to put in, to pay the price, you will eventually enjoy rewards out of all proportion to your efforts.

More than that, you'll become a person of character and competence, of pride and self-respect. You'll become the kind of person you always dreamed you would become, the kind that others look up to and admire.

CHAPTER 7

SETTING OUT

The distance from London to Gibraltar is approximately 1,600 miles by the shortest route. Allowing for our inexperience with traveling long distances by bicycle, we optimistically reckoned that we could average 80 miles a day. That would put us in Gibraltar by the end of April. However, there were several variables we failed to take into consideration—the first and worst being the hills located directly in our line of travel.

We covered 30 miles on the first day of that terrible trip to Gibraltar, collapsing in an irrigation ditch south of London, exhausted and famished, just before sundown. Our legs were rubbery with fatigue, and we smelled of sweat and exhaust fumes, our hair dried like straw and our faces streaked with dirt and grime. The day had been a battle from the first flat tire, but we had won, and surely, we thought, tomorrow would be a good deal easier.

Cautiously, worried about being arrested for trespassing, we built a lean-to with our ground sheet and camouflaged it with twigs and grass, hiding our bicycles in the bushes nearby. We managed to work an element of drama into everything we did, proceeding as though there was a plot afoot to thwart our adventure. We assumed that people would look at us when we went into stores to buy food, and say under their breaths to their friends, "I wonder where those young men with the air of mystery are going!"

It is more likely, though, that they said something like, "Bums! Every year, more and more bums on the road. What's the country coming to?"

After a supper of bread and cheese, followed by Geoff's tea made over a smoky fire, we sat wearily for a few minutes and then, by common assent, crawled into the bags and slept. Tomorrow would surely be better.

In the morning, we woke stiff and cold, dirty and hungry. It took two hours of pedaling to work the pain out of our thighs and shoulders. Geoff said something like, "Muscle ache means muscle development," in an attempt at encouragement. Bob and I refused to speak to him for the next 10 miles.

And the hunger! Until you've sweated yourself sick with pain and lack of nourishment on a bicycle, you don't know what hunger is! We stopped in the evenings trembling with weakness and woke in the mornings from the knife twisted into our empty bellies. Once we stopped at a cafe for breakfast and ate the entire menu twice. After that, we couldn't trust ourselves in places selling hot food, forcing the buying of supplies for supper and breakfast at small grocery stores. The all-consuming hunger was a constant companion, never far away. It was another factor we had not taken into consideration when we chose bicycles.

Three days after saying good-bye to Aunt Barbara, we rode into Dover and along the White Cliffs to the ferry terminal. On the way to Calais, we thumbed through our French-English dictionary, looking up and writing down words we thought we would need. We soon learned that the travel book tenet "Everyone speaks English" was wrong. No member of the crew on the ferry spoke any English, and living as close to the land as we were, we realized that a knowledge of French was not only an asset, it was a necessity. We rode from the extreme north of France to the extreme south and never met a single Frenchman who spoke English. I guess they hadn't read the same travel books!

The good news was that I had begun studying French in earnest back in Montreal in October. My understanding and eventual fluency in the language as we drove deeper into Africa proved to be a valuable asset. It may have saved our lives as well.

I later learned that *the biggest mental block to learning a new language, or any other skill, is the fear of looking or sounding foolish during the time between unfamiliarity and mastery.* A rule that has served me all my life is this: *What is worth doing is worth doing poorly at first, and often it's worth doing poorly several times.*

The power is always on the side of the person with superior knowledge and skills. The law of Requisite Variety says that, "In any group of people, the individual having the highest integrated level of knowledge and skill will tend to rise to dominate and lead all other individuals in that group."

The good news is that *you can learn anything you need to learn to achieve any goal you set for yourself. Your personal boundaries are determined more by inner limitations than by outer circumstances.* The only real limits on your potential are the ones you impose on yourself by your own thinking.

NEW SITUATIONS REQUIRE NEW ATTITUDES

Frustrated expectations lie at the root of most unhappiness. To survive and thrive in new situations, you must keep your mind open and be willing to question your expectations.

The good news is that you are extremely adaptable to change and variety. You can learn to cope with any situation, if you decide to.

One of the most helpful exercises you can do is to separate "facts" from "problems." A fact is just like the weather. It cannot be altered. You don't waste a minute of energy or emotion railing against "facts." You just accept them and get on with your life.

A "problem," however, is different. It is a situation that is amenable to a solution. It is something you can do something about.

The key to happiness, success, and personal power is for you to focus on the future, on solutions to the problems you can do something about.

And remember, you can learn anything you need to learn to achieve any goal you set for yourself.

CHAPTER 8

OUR TOUR DE FRANCE

April in France can be very lovely, I am sure. Through the sweat and rain of those arduous days, I glimpsed many indications of a wonderful potential. The promise of summer was everywhere in the rolling green hills, the early buttercups along the grassy shoulders, the swallows singing, flying in from the south. However, the gusting winds and intermittent rains that swept across the open road, drenching and sending their piercing chills through our thin jeans and down our uncovered necks, were a reminder that winter was not long past and summer was not yet here.

The roads don't follow the lay of the land because the hills are not high, and it was obviously more practical to build them straight from town to town, over hills and plains with very few curves to offset their directness. A motorist in northern France can thus make very good time between towns and over long distances. And the roads are, of course, built for motorists.

On a bicycle it is a different bucket of sweat altogether. The law of averages says that for every amount of uphill there must be an equal and opposite amount of downhill, but somehow it didn't seem to work out that way on the roads we travelled. The time we lost on the ascent, we should have recovered on the descent. But more often than not, the downhill rides were into the wind. And, if the descent was gradual, it would be as difficult as pedaling on a level stretch.

I learned later in life that, *in any new venture, the roads are all uphill, and the wind is always in your face.* Murphy's Laws apply with a vengeance: "Anything that can go wrong will go wrong. Of all the things that can go wrong, the worst possible thing will go wrong at the worst possible time and cost the greatest amount of money." Murphy was our constant companion.

As we approached the upgrades, we'd pedal furiously in third gear, then second, then first, the thrusts coming slower and slower, the muscles along the tops of the thighs burning, the breaths coming in painful gasps. The forward momentum would cease before we jumped off and pushed the bikes up the rest of the way, arriving at the top pouring with sweat. Often we were strung out over a mile, and we used the hilltops as places to stop until the third man came up. Then we'd remount the bikes and attack the next hill, hour after hour, doggedly trying to make a reasonable average.

Exhausted as we were each night, we slept long and soundly in forests and fields along the road, despite the rain and discomfort. Around 10 a.m. we would break camp and get back on our bicycles, stiff but rested, and always in good spirits. The refreshed feeling and the good spirits would last until the third hill, after which it was just determined slogging and unending miles of hard work. The stiffness abated by noon, only to come seeping back shortly after, and stay with us for the duration of the day's ride.

The wet, windswept road became an enemy to be conquered. The diminishing distances between us and the towns ahead became our measures of victory and achievement. We had soon realized that bicycles were not the ideal solution to our transportation problems, but we had named our poison and neither the road nor the bicycles were going to defeat us. We were the Bon Vivants, we were undefeatable, and we were going to Africa.

If those cold, windy, pain-wracked days were some of the worst of our lives, they were some of the best, too. When we stopped in the last afternoon to camp, usually in small clumps of trees not far off the road, the first thing we did was to build a fire, and the second thing was to open the wine purchased in the last town. The fire would warm our faces and dry our clothes, and the wine took care of the rest. By the time supper was cooked, the magic warmth of the wine would tingle its happy way into our tired brains and back down again, flowing through our bodies like music, erasing the day in its soothing passage. With the dinner eaten and the fire crackling and dancing, a peace and joyous content would settle over our camp. We'd laugh and loaf and dream and feel truly sorry for anyone who could never feel as wonderfully happy and as genuinely fulfilled as we.

I have learned that there is a fine line between the best of times and the worst of times, between pleasure and pain, joy and sorrow.

We couldn't afford to stay in hotels, and after a few nights of camping, we had no interest in anywhere but the element we had chosen—that of cool crisp nights and happy hours, of laughter unto tears, of unspeakable joy. Never had we been so robust and easy to laugh, never had we eaten so well and enjoyed it so much, never had our nights been so restful and so much appreciated. The camping in the evenings almost made us forget the conditions of the day that made it so treasured.

But then came the mornings, and breakfast, and another day of stinging sweat and aching backs. I guess the intensity of the pleasure of the wine-soaked evenings by the little fires was only made possible by the grueling labor and pain of the long days that preceded them.

We must have looked a bit unusual as we made our way across the farm country, through tiny villages, our faces unshaven, machetes jutting out of our bulging rucksacks. Often people came to their windows and doors to follow us silently with their eyes, watching our passing until we were far down the road, before returning to what they had been doing.

When we stopped to buy food in the larger towns, we were often asked where we were from and where we were going, and when they learned that our destination was Africa, they would say that Africa was very far, or very hot, or very dangerous, but they always seemed to approve. No matter why we were going there, people liked the idea that we were going somewhere else, as if the going was an answer to something.

I learned later that *people will often encourage you in a risky venture as long as it means nothing to them.* If you invited them to come along, it would be a different thing. In life and in business, *the acid test is to invite them to invest their own money.* Then you learn how deep their approval goes.

Our route was laid out as the shortest distance between London and Gibraltar, since even a few miles of difference in one route, as opposed to another, meant extra hours of toil. We rode south to Boulogne, then to Abbeville, and on through Beauvais to Chartres on the eighth day of pedaling.

After cashing a traveler's check in a small bank in Chartres, we sat down on the curb outside to assess our position. It was not encouraging. The wind, rain, hunger, muscular aches, and pains had all combined to keep our speed so low that we were only averaging 40 miles a day. From the original $1,000, we had only $750 left, and we still had a long way to go to Gibraltar.

The bicycles and equipment had cost a lot, but what was gobbling our funds was the price of food. Although we were limiting ourselves to two large meals per day, those meals had to be enormous and nutritious. Meat, eggs, cheese, bread, milk and vegetables for three ravenous fellows was inordinately expensive in France, even though we were buying carefully. At our rate of speed, we couldn't possibly finish the first part of our trip in less than another four weeks, and by that time we'd be very low on cash.

What really upset us was a genial motorcyclist, an American, who stopped to chat with us. It turned out that he had left London that morning and covered the same ground in eight hours that we had covered in five days. We smiled through our tears.

I learned later that *a person who knows what he or she is doing can cover greater distance faster and easier than the most determined but inexperienced person can cover under the same circumstance.* This is why businesses started by experienced entrepreneurs have a 90 percent success rate, while businesses started by inexperienced people fail 90 percent of the time. There is simply no replacement for having done it before, for knowledge and experience.

We calculated that it would be cheaper to take a train than to continue on bicycles. Once into the south of France, we hoped the wind would be gone and the weather would be considerably more pleasant for bicycling. We would make better time and enjoy the traveling, something we were having a rather tough time doing in the rain.

To save money and justify taking a train instead of sticking it out in the rain, we made ourselves a deal. It was then noon; if we could be in Orleans, 71 kilometers further south, in time to catch the 10:25 southbound train from Paris that night, we would have earned the train ride and there would be nothing on our consciences.

"How's that for an idea, fellows?"

"What?"

"Oh, come on now, it's not that far."

"Yes, I know. I'm just as tired as you are."

"It's a matter of pride, that's why."

Anyway, we all agreed that it was a fine idea and started for Orleans. We had already bicycled 20 kilometers that day, and the rain hadn't let up for a second.

All afternoon we punished ourselves, pedaling into the icy wind, knuckles white on the handlebars from the cold, eyes narrowed against the lash of the fine spray, chests burning with the exertion, and legs screaming silently from the pain that gradually spread up into the back and shoulders and slithered down into the wrists. Our jeans were soaked through. We were chilled to the bone. But there was no way to justify a stop and no place to stop, if we could justify it. The hours marched by with the milestones, jeering at our creeping pace: 40 kilometers from Orleans, and we were on our last legs; 30 kilometers to go, and we no longer dared to stop at the top of the hills for fear our exhausted bodies would refuse to continue. We would reach the end of the upgrades and just keep on trudging with the bicycles until we had enough breath to throw our legs over and take up the silent count of pedal strokes once more.

Twenty kilometers to go, and we knew there was no stopping us. Ignoring the incessant honking of passing motorists as the bikes wandered into the road, ignoring the hollow twisting knots of hunger in the gut, ignoring everything but the road directly in front of the wheel, like silent, relentless robots we forced the hateful pedals down.

Just after dusk, a yellow Citroen passed us, beeping its horn as it sped by, then slowing and stopping on the road ahead. As we rode our bedraggled way past the car, a man got out and motioned for us to stop.

Unable to get off our bikes, we straddled them weakly and waited to hear his troubles. He was very gracious and led us to understand that he lived in Orleans, and would take our gear in with him to make our loads a little lighter.

We nodded in mute agreement and dropped the bicycles unceremoniously in the street in our fumbling haste to throw our things into the opened trunk. There was no discussion about honest intentions or ulterior motives. We thanked him and stood watching as his car disappeared into the night. Stuffing the address into his pocket, Geoff picked up his bike and climbed on wordlessly. We followed suit and began the silent cadence once more.

When you're at wits end, your load no longer bearable, amazingly some bit of relief will come to your aid. The burden remains, but at least you can continue.

Because of our hunger and mind-numbing fatigue, the last 10 kilometers were lost in a haze of signs and arrows pointing toward "Orleans-Centre Ville." Every muscle in our bodies felt as though it were being held in place with a hot spike. The rain had stopped, and the moisture over the road and electric wires caught the lights from oncoming cars, sparkling clear against the blackness of the fields. It was like riding through an alley of flashing pain and stunning motion until the road suddenly widened into four lanes and poured out into the square in the center of town.

The main street through the square was ablaze with lights and music, honking horns and the flashing headlights reflecting against the rain-damp roads and the row of gaily lit restaurants lining the boulevard. Glasses tinkled and laughter echoed from table to table, the white-uniformed waiters gliding in and out with overfilled trays, the jukeboxes blaring into the crowds surging along the broad sidewalks. We stopped at the corner of the street where the entire panorama of light and excitement began and stretched for several blocks. Stolidly we stared with glazed eyes, taking it all in happily.

It was 5:30. We had made it to Orleans on time, but we felt like the survivors of a massacre.

At that moment, one of the boys who had been in the back seat of the Citroen rode up on his bicycle, enthusiastically motioning us to follow him. We were halfway off our bikes in the direction of the nearest cafe, numb with exhaustion and giddy from hunger, and the suggestion that we delay eating to retrieve our equipment was greeted with scowls. The boy, however, insisted, assuring us that it wasn't far. Like robots we heaved our stiffening limbs onto the bikes and pedaled away from the lights onto a dark side street.

It was two blocks to a featureless three-story house in a tightly constructed row of similar buildings whose front doors opened onto the narrow sidewalk. At the boy's eager knock, the door was opened, and we were ushered inside by the bespectacled gentleman who had relieved us of our gear three hours before.

In sharp contrast to the dull facade, the entrance hall was lined with mirrors, the walls of the parlor and dining room done in white fresco depicting spring landscapes, cherubim and angels. The furniture was of black walnut, richly polished and situated elegantly around a high fireplace. Above the burnished walnut table in the dining room, a crystal chandelier dangled on a silver chain. And the most memorable part of the whole scene was the fragrant aromas floating in from the kitchen beyond the dining room.

Monsieur Allo was a pleasant businessman, well-mannered, and sure that we would like a little something to eat after our ride. While his wife was busy in the kitchen, he invited us to seat our emaciated selves around the long table and tell him and his sons about our trip.

Pasting "hands across the seamanship" smiles on our grubby, unshaven faces, we laboriously used what words of French we knew, and let them deduce the meaning. All we could think of was the food. Every distant sound from the kitchen was a clarion call of forthcoming joy.

The movement finally stopped in the kitchen, and the door swung open as Madame Allo swept into the dining room with a cheery smile. As we caught our breaths in anticipation, she leaned over and set a bowl of soup in the middle of the table. I didn't know whether to laugh or cry.

Our first nourishment in 11 hours and 91 kilometers consisted of a medium-sized tureen of thin celery soup, and a two-inch diameter loaf of French bread sliced into bite-size chunks. Any one of us could have devoured the lot, but it was for all of us, including the family of four.

The soup plates were carefully distributed by the younger son and Madame Allo elegantly ladled out a dipper full into each bowl. Through gritted teeth, we made an effort not to slurp the soup down our fronts as we hurriedly spooned it into our screaming innards, resisting the impulse to pick up the bowl in both hands and gobble the thin contents.

Our ill-concealed hopes were in vain; the soup was not an entrée. It was the alpha and the omega. After waiting long enough to ascertain that there was to be nothing more, we said our good-byes and edged toward the door, shouldering our packs and grinning insincerely. As the door closed behind us, the grins disappeared in a hasty scramble for our bikes.

Battle stations! Into the main street and up to the first bistro we skidded, leading the confused waiter to the table and explaining in desperate French what we wanted. Half an hour later the table was littered with empty plates, and we were out of critical condition. With a little sleep, our chances for recovery seemed quite good.

The beefsteak and potatoes had stopped the hollow ache in our stomachs and rekindled a little energy, which we directed into drinking a bottle of "vin ordinaire" and watching the passing parade on the busy sidewalk. The wine soon smothered the spark of energy from the food, and the long day began to catch up with us, our heads nodding and conversation dropping to broken, meaningless sentences. We paid the bill and dragged across the square to the Orleans main train station, checking the bikes with the baggage department after buying the tickets, and then sat on the empty platform where our train was supposed to appear.

It was right on time. Knowing nothing about the French railways, and thinking only of sleeping, we clambered into the last car and shut ourselves into the end compartment. Since few other passengers boarded the train, we hoped to sleep through the night while traveling. When the train started out of the station, the car was still empty. We congratulated ourselves on our luck and stretched out on the padded seats to sleep.

But, 11 minutes after leaving the station, the train jerked to a halt, stirring Geoff and me from our half-slumbering positions on opposite benches of the narrow compartment. Irritably we raised our heads above the level of the window and peered out. At a platform about 10 yards away, we saw a long, brightly lit passenger train, full of milling, laughing people crowding in and out of busy compartments.

"I'm glad we're not on that train," Geoff mumbled, and withdrew his head. The snoring emitting from the next compartment indicated that Bob was beyond giving an opinion. I also withdrew my head and laid down again.

Seconds later, the door to the next compartment opened and a gruff French voice demanded something of the sleeping Bob. He woke and mumbled incomprehensibly. Thinking that it must be someone wanting to see our tickets, I took them in, followed closely by Geoff.

The bulky, blue-uniformed, whiskered conductor seemed to be of the opinion that Bob should not be on this train, and when we entered, blinking at the brighter light, he included us in his protests. He was babbling furiously in French, gesticulating toward the door and the platform, and we could understand nothing more than that he was interrupting our sleep with his chatter.

I showed him the tickets for Toulouse to placate him, but he merely punched them and handed them back, still talking and suggesting vociferously that we were not in the right compartment. He insisted that we get off the train. Just as loudly, we told him that we were staying. After a last burst of French, he stepped onto the platform and strode away indignantly.

"What was all that about?"

"Don't know. Don't care either. He was probably trying to get us onto another car, so he'd have this for someone who tips better."

"Well, he can drop dead. We're here and we're staying."

"Geez, I'm beat. Wake me up when we get to Toulouse."

We switched off the lights and laid back on our respective benches. Outside, we could hear the other train pulling away and clacking off into the night. Seconds later, our train also began to move—backward in the same direction from which we'd come.

"It's going back," said Geoff, without raising his head.

"No it's not. It's just transferring to another line for the trip to Toulouse."

After a brief silence, Geoff raised his head to look out the window, staring intently.

"We're passing the same refinery that we passed coming out," he said, as a matter of interest.

"Can't be. Must be some other refinery. There are probably lots of refineries around Orleans."

"There's the bus terminal, too," he said. "We must be going back."

"Maybe they've forgotten our bicycles. Yeah, that must be it. They've forgotten our bicycles."

Three minutes later, the train pulled back into the huge, brightly lit dome of the Orleans main station, coming to a halt exactly where we had boarded it. We lay silently in the dark, listening to the voices on the platform outside, half asleep and uncaring. Five minutes later the train again moved out of the station into the darkness of the rail yards.

"That must have been it," said Geoff drowsily. "We seem to be on our way again. Funny they should forget a bicycle."

Again we dozed as the train clattered along under the bridges, past the bus terminal, past the refinery, and out into the suburbs, jerking to a halt 11 minutes later at the same platform as before. Only this time there was no other train, no conductor, no one at all. Just the rain and the night and the lonely lights of the deserted transfer station. Eight minutes later we sat up when the train started back in the same direction, and watched dopily out the window at the passing landmarks: past the refinery, past the bus terminal, under the bridges, and across the rail yards to the main station. The truth, the bitter truth, dawned on us.

We were on a shuttle train! The other train had been the southbound from Paris on the way to Toulouse. The little conductor had been trying to tell us that we must change trains.

We learned that the next train headed south didn't come through until the next morning at 7:30. It was raining again, it was late, and we were very, very tired. There was only one solution. After a brief conference, we decided to sleep right where we were on the shuttle train.

All night the train rumbled out of the station to the little platform in the suburbs, stopped for eight minutes, and rumbled back, while we slept fitfully to the rocking motion in the darkened compartment.

Occasionally, when the train would stop at the station, one of us would climb out and go into the men's washroom on the adjacent platform. Minutes later, he would come out, give a sleepy nod to the curious members of the terminal staff working through the night, and reboard before the train rolled out of the station once more. As the night wore on, they began to expect us; and they would always be watching when someone got off, which amused them no end. It seemed that sort of thing wasn't done too often in Orleans.

I learned that *sometimes the very best thing you can do in a difficult situation is—nothing. Just accept the situation as it is and bide your time. Your chance will come.*

The next morning, Sunday, somewhat refreshed after a moderately comfortable night and right on schedule, we boarded the southbound train to Toulouse and once more continued on our way to Gibraltar. The train wasn't crowded, and we easily found an almost empty compartment where we could sit and watch the hills go by. We shaved and washed in the cramped toilets, and arrived in Limoges that afternoon.

The weather was better already, the day sparkling clear, the sky dotted with puffy white cumulus clouds sweeping by on a pale blue carpet. We had one hour to wait in Limoges for the connection to Toulouse. It was a good chance to look at a few buildings, as well as find a place to eat. We joined families strolling on the quiet boulevards, reveling in the warm spring sunshine as we made our way into town. The streets were deserted, the stores were shut tight for the weekend, and there wasn't a place to eat anywhere.

Half a mile of undernourished searching into the city, after a gradual ascent of several blocks, we came into a colorful square built around a fountain. Spreading from the base of the fountain in the shape of a star were five little gardens swollen with red and yellow flowers, the points of the stars aimed at restaurants facing onto the square. And from the aromas wafting into the clear air, we figured they were open for business.

"What are we waiting for?"

"Who's waiting?"

"Which one looks the cheapest?"

"That one."

"Well, what are we waiting for?"

"Who's waiting?"

We sat down and ordered a four-course lunch on the understanding with the waiter that we were in a hurry, since our train pulled out in 30 minutes, and the next one wasn't until the following morning. The waiter nodded vigorously with a smile of perfect rapport when we explained that we must be back to the terminal by 2 p.m. Fingers flipping with a show of efficiency, he glided away to the big kitchen in the rear.

After five minutes, I got up and went to the door of the kitchen. The waiter was sitting at a table reading a newspaper. He looked up, mildly interested at my entrance.

"We must catch a train in 30 minutes," I told him, and then repeated the same message two or three ways so he would be sure to understand. "Bring the food to the table all at once, please. We are in a hurry."

"Oui, oui, messieur," he said. "It is coming immediately, if you will go and sit and wait."

With a burst of professionalism, he followed me back to the table with a large tureen of thin vegetable soup. Ceremoniously, as though it was the solution for everything, he set it in the center of the table and wandered nonchalantly to the mirrored bar, where he began chatting with the bartender.

By this time, we had less than 20 minutes before we would be stuck in Limoges for the night. Tersely, we called him back to the table and told him to bring all the food, NOW.

With a look of surprise that we should want another course when we were still slurping the soup, he hurried into the kitchen and hurried back, this time with a large salad bowl. Rolling his eyes as though we had just sworn in church, he walked over to the window and sat down, staring into the square aimlessly.

"More! More!" we shouted, "Bring more! Bring it all!"

Grossly offended, the waiter again came to the table. This time I held up the menu and then my watch. "If we don't have it *all* in another two minutes, we'll have to leave to catch our train—and we're not paying," I told him.

He'd never heard anything so blasphemous in his whole life. But, he hurried off to the kitchen and came back with the next course.

The minutes were running out, and we still wanted more. We dashed through the second half of the meal, eating with both hands, paid the bill, and streaked into the street. Far away a train whistle sounded high and clear.

We sprinted across the square and down the cobbled street, cutting across a newly planted lawn. Gasping and perspiring on our full stomachs, we dove through hedges and galloped along sidewalks, causing women pushing baby strollers to leap aside. Finishing with a quarter-mile run down the center of the city park, bloated and puffing, we tore across the parking lot and bolted through the wide swinging doors of the train station. People turned to stare in curious incredulity as we dodged and sidestepped our way down the busy hall, swung through the turnstile, and plunged down three levels of stairs to the platform below.

The train had just started to move. We peeled off like jet fighters, spacing ourselves. Scooping up our waiting rucksacks as we ran, we sprinted straight for the last car. I was the first inside; Bob dove in after me as the train gained speed. Geoff was now in a full sprint down the platform. We shouted at him to run faster. With a final burst of speed, he grabbed my outstretched hand and tossed his pack to Bob, who literally dragged him onboard just as the train soared out of the station.

Completely spent, we lay on the floor, gasping for a full five minutes before anyone spoke. Then Bob sagely observed, "We almost missed the train."

Yes, that seemed to be a safe assumption. Were there any more clever children like him at home? Perhaps they'd be good enough to stay there.

We found an empty compartment and rode comfortably the remainder of the way to Toulouse.

I learned later that most people, like the waiter, are not particularly ambitious, for a variety of reasons, and that *no one places the same value on your time as you do.* Only about 2 percent of people have a "sense of urgency," and they end up at the top of any organization. Just making a firm personal commitment to "do it now," to operate in "real time," can give you the winning edge in almost any competitive situation.

"It's easy to fight when everything's right," says the poet, and it certainly seemed appropriate when we came off that train in Toulouse. It was late afternoon, and the sky was glistening with golden rays of warmth. The clouds were left behind in the Loire Valley, and the road ran toward the south under a sky we knew was Mediterranean. We could almost smell the orange blossoms and salt spray from the railroad station.

Like young tigers, we leaped on our bicycles and pedaled out of town, following the signs to Carcassone and the sea, full of confidence, power, youth, and joy in the birds and flowers and the glorious world of excitement and adventure. The electricity of delight tingled down our hardening limbs, lightening our wind-burned faces with laughter and happiness, our hearts brimming with song and springtime.

The knowledge that we were conquerors, and unstoppable, leaped and danced in our tumbling brains, warming us with pride and hope and defiance. What did we care for the elements, for the rain and the cold? We were lovers in a field of flowers, eager to pluck the waving blossoms of beckoning experience, to hurl defiance at everything and anything that stood in the way of our trip to Africa. We were unquenchable drinkers at the fountain of dreams and romance, insatiable eaters at the table of rugged living and challenge. It was a long way to Tipperary, but in our imaginations and hearts, we were on the highroad, and halfway back already.

In those fancy-free days, we almost welcomed the wind and the rain, seeing in them an opportunity to flaunt our dauntlessness, there in France, far from home and love and security; we were explorers and discoverers, poets and lovers, Bon Vivants and vagabonds supreme. With each drop of sweat and each painful gasp, we were taking part in the battle of youth against age, the conflict between the lure of the easy chair and the lone trail. We felt genuinely sorry for people speeding past in their cars, saddened that they couldn't share our labors and revel in the satisfaction of tired bodies and kinship with the hard life. We were giving the best we had in stamina and determination, heeding the call of distant places, striking the words "quit" and "defeat" from our vocabularies.

We were three idealistic boys, painting drama and romance around commonplace occurrences, looking for and finding the mysterious in everything new or unusual. We thought of ourselves as exceptional people for having taken up the gauntlet of Africa when others our age were contenting themselves with bumming around Europe. We wanted something more, but we didn't have the slightest idea what it was. We thought it was Africa, and so that vast unknown land mass became our Mecca, and the bicycles our penance and pilgrimage.

We rode another two hours that afternoon, to a little place called Montgiscard, where we searched for a place to buy the evening meal and breakfast. But we had miscalculated again; it was Sunday night, and nothing was open.

As a last resort, we halted at a wayside café to ask if they would sell us a few provisions. The owner was a large motherly woman who took one look at us and our bicycles and adopted us without another word. She took us into her warm, homey kitchen and loaded us with bread, eggs, milk, onions, and tomatoes. At her friendly insistence, we made our camp on the hill above the café, cooking the egg-and-onion omelet over a smoky fire set in the roots of a spreading oak.

The night fell sharp and chilly after supper, with a light breeze running under the groundsheet we had rigged up as an open tent. The warmth and music floating from the café below drew us like a magnet off the muddy hill.

Business in the café was good, and the atmosphere was even better. Most of the light came from the bright bar in one corner and the jukebox next to it. Mama was bustling back and forth from the kitchen to the guests at the bar. She was a bundle of happy efficiency, enjoying her role as hostess like a queen at a coronation. She greeted us and introduced us to the crowd cheerily, then led us to a table and presented us with a bottle of wine. Joining the mostly older crowd, farm folk from the area, in the restaurant, we felt caught up in the music and good spirits of the establishment. The dancing and laughter in the dim gaiety had us feeling like members of a homecoming party.

We drank Mama's bottle of wine, and one more, before making our way back up the hill. That night we slept through the rain that soaked our fireplace and half our gear. We could have slept through a blizzard.

Monday morning dawned clear and windy, the wind coming out of the north for the first time. With breakfast and good-byes taken care of, we were on the road, making exceptional time. The wind often was so strong at our backs that we had no need to pedal. All that day we rode like fools, effortlessly, the tires singing on the tarmac. Into the rolling hills and vineyards, through Castelnaudery, then Carcassone, then down to the Mediterranean at Narbonne, joyously we flew ahead of the crisp gusts of winds.

At Narbonne, we bought our daily groceries and continued along the coast toward Spain until we found an old Roman watch-tower and set up camp inside for the night.

That was the best day we had ever had on bicycles, covering 140 kilometers without the exhaustion that had marked days when we had only travelled 60 or 70. I'm glad we had that day, not only because we deserved it, but also because it showed us, just once, how pleasurable traveling on a bicycle can be. We needed that one glorious day to temper the memory of the hard days past and to boost us in the days ahead.

THERE ARE NO FREE LESSONS

Nature is a just employer, but she demands full measure of payment for every reward. The trials and tribulations of our bicycling trip across France forced us to draw deep into ourselves for reserves of energy and patience.

The good news is that *your biggest problem or difficulty today has been sent to you at this moment to teach you something you need to know to be happier and more successful in the future.*

It is when you are experiencing the greatest pain and strain that you are often preparing for the greatest joys and pleasures.

Develop an "attitude of gratitude." Count your blessings. Look for the good in every situation and surprise. You'll always find it.

CHAPTER 9

THE SPANISH RAILWAYS

The next day, although the wind changed again, we entered the foothills of the Pyrenees before camping the night just beyond Perpignan. On Wednesday morning, we got another passport stamp at the Spanish border station of Le Perthus and began the long haul to Barcelona.

In life, everything is cycles and trends, upwards and downwards, better and then worse, progressing and regressing. Nothing ever continues indefinitely in the same way. It's a matter of two steps forward, one back, and sometimes more than one step back. That's why *the best way to predict the future is sometimes to create it.*

"Africa begins at the Pyrenees" was said a long time ago, probably by someone who'd been to both and liked neither. One thing we could attest to by the time we rode into the soot-blackened outskirts of Barcelona three days later, teeth rattling, was that the bad roads begin at the Pyrenees. If anyone ever gets up a protest march against cobblestones, save me a banner to carry!

A check at Poste Restaunte, the General Delivery of Europe and the rest of the world, freed us from any obligation to answer letters, since those who knew we were going through there had either run out of ink, or thought we wouldn't make it. We contented ourselves with finding a cheap place to stay the weekend.

For 42 pesetas each, per night, we found a small pension whose owners were not overly concerned with encouraging the tourist trade. Our quarters consisted of a converted closet with two sagging beds shoved together, one water spigot with a tin bowl for washing and shaving, and a large window opening onto a roof overlooking an impoverished neighborhood.

For five pesetas and a half-hour wait, we could get enough hot water out of the old electric tank in the distant bathroom to brush our teeth, if we were inclined toward that sort of thing. However, all our clothes had become caked and filthy after 10 days of sleeping in them at night, and sweating in them during the day, so we took advantage of the deluxe facilities to wash them.

The wash was accompanied by the wails and protestations of the derelict from the desk, who repeatedly threatened to call the police if we didn't leave immediately and wash our clothes some- where else. He finally went away.

The flies that seemed to cluster on us when we stopped in the streets, or even slowed, indicated that a little bathing wouldn't hurt us either. After we'd scraped off a little dirt with a carbolic soap, our room, when we were in it, stopped smelling as though a rat had died in the woodwork.

We had arrived in the morning and were feeling quite like men of the world in our clean dry clothes that afternoon. We felt it only fair that since the Spaniards had built this city in our way, we go out and give it the once over, especially since it was Good Friday.

The streets had been quiet all day but were now coming to life. Long rows and clusters of chairs were being set up on the main boulevards and sidewalks. People dressed in their Sunday finery were pouring into the large streets from the many smaller ones lead- ing away from the center of town. The stores were closed, except those dealing in soft drinks and pastry, and the pious looks on the faces of the solemn Spaniards left no doubt but that they took their religious holidays seriously.

Gradually the multitudes of chairs filled and overflowed with the multitudes of Spaniards, the streets becoming packed and swarming around them. We felt like outsiders, partly because we weren't overly moved by the occasion, and largely because of the scowls that the better-dressed natives were giving us. Our jeans and T-shirts did not lend much to the holiness of the occasion.

We concentrated more on catching the eyes of the Spanish damsels, receiving more than one blush or smile in return. But we could not meet them, as they were surrounded by parents and jeal- ous brothers. When they sat beautifully in their spring dresses, the family group extended its tentacles of protection to the front, sides, and rear of the lovely creatures. When they walked, it was invari- ably with Mama and Papa on either arm, and often a brother or cousin bringing up the rear. It was a bit discouraging for us to walk around Spain's second largest city, steeped in lascivious thoughts but unable to do more than lust. Alas, that was part of the cross we had to bear to become world-beaters.

Early the next morning, we got our bicycles and rode through the quiet streets, to the outskirts along the waterfront. No packs this time. This was to be a pleasure tour of the low spots, and some of them were pretty low. Once away from the main streets, we got into slum areas consisting of clumps of shanties held together with chicken wire, built from cardboard and tin sheets.

I remember thinking to myself that these were probably the worst conditions I'd ever seen and that it was good for us to see; it broadened our education. Little did I know what awaited in Africa.

On Easter morning we pedaled off toward Valencia and right into the wind once more. It was another day of counted pumps, burning thighs and eyes full of fine grit from the sand between the cobbles; another day of sweat and gritted teeth. The pack straps dug into our shoulders with the constant joggling and rattling of the rough road, our stomachs knotted from hunger, our hands on the lowered handle bars became stiff and cramped. All the rigors and tribulations of bicycling set in once more.

One day. Two days. Three days. The wind became the enemy and the enemy was vicious. It never let up. It lurked at every bend in the road, attacking us up and down every hill, slashing our faces with sand. It gave us no peace and no quarter; at night it took almost an hour to cook the egg-and-onion omelets as the little fires struggled to stay alive. The wind shook us wrathfully awake every morning, drove at us all day, and howled angrily to keep us awake throughout the night.

We grew to hate the wind, and the road and the bicycles that were part of the ceaseless ordeal. Outside Tarragona the wind became so strong that maximum effort was required just to keep from being blown over in a standstill. After four days we were barely a two-hour drive out of Barcelona, and at last the wind won.

It was after a breakfast of egg (the cheapest protein) and onions (the only vegetable available that early in the year) omelet (the easiest to prepare) in a rocky creek bed with the wind whistling up the rocks from the road below that we finally decided to reevaluate our situation.

"We're like fools banging our heads against a brick wall," said Geoff, "because it'll feel so good when we stop. I say we should stop now!"

"If I never ride another bicycle in my life, it'll be too soon," agreed Bob, resolutely.

"But think how tough we're getting with this life."

"Yeah, well I'm tough enough already."

"Yes, but it's a matter of pride."

"What do you mean?"

"If we quit now, think how much tougher it'll be to carry on when it gets tough in the future."

"Who's thinking about the future?"

"Well, I'm thinking about the future."

"Let's try it for another three days."

"The hell with it!"

"What about two days?"

"Oh, come on, at least one day more."

"Hey, fellows, you're not even listening. Let's discuss this."

"What's that? Vinaroz. The next town? Now slow down for just one second!"

"Where are you two going? Hold on a minute. Let's not rush off without thinking this over."

"Yes, but we haven't thought it over enough."

"Let's take a vote! Aw, for cripes sakes, wait for me!" And with that dialogue, off we went to the train station.

Sometimes in business and in life you have to try, try again and then try something else. Remember: "Difficulties come not to obstruct, but to instruct." Always be prepared to adapt, adjust and respond by doing something else.

Pains and Trains

Vinaroz was a typical Spanish town: streets lined with box-like clay and brick houses, except in the center, where the larger buildings rose two or three stories. Other than a mangy goat nibbling at a bit of dusty grass, the depot by the tracks at the end of town seemed deserted.

We rode across the unpaved yard to the old frame building and stomped around inside, calling hopefully, until an old man wearing the remains of a blue overcoat stuck his head through one of the barred ticket windows. Grudgingly, he growled the prices at us and then sold us third-class tickets to Valencia before going back to sleep. We had two hours to wait and set off to find something to eat, our universal remedy for all ailments, including riding, walking, sitting, and delays caused by Spanish trains.

After eating an overpriced something in a sidewalk greasy spoon, we passed the next hour soaking up a little local culture before pedaling back early enough not to miss the train. We were not the only ones who were early.

In the previously empty yard in front of the tracks was gathered a multitude that Moses would have been proud to lead. There were old men in peasant clothing, unshaved and sweat stained, accompanied by old women dressed in the ubiquitous black of mourning, popular throughout Spain. There were tired-looking husbands and wives, tending bundles of family possessions and underfed children. There were young men and ancient farmers in the crowd, the yard cluttered with goats, chickens, dogs, mattresses, babies, baskets, vegetables, and old bicycles. Now, there were also three scruffy-looking gringos to make the party complete.

Everyone sat in the hot, dry sun of mid-afternoon and looked tiredly at everyone else, as though waiting for a hearse to pass. A few heads turned to look at us when we rode up, and after assuring themselves that we didn't bite, returned to staring resignedly at the dust. We gave our bicycles over to the bandit at the baggage counter and took our place with the others.

Moses arrived, in the form of a coal-blackened, greasy-looking engineer, running the old steam engine that dragged the converted cattle cars into Vinaroz 15 minutes late. His inspirational powers were astonishing; all trace of lazy Spanish peasant dissolved in a mad, squalling, chaotic rush to get aboard. We hurled ourselves into the thick of it, yelling and pushing with the best of them, scrambling for places for our packs and sleeping bags in the narrow compartments. The corridors quickly filled with humanity, just as the old engine gave one shrill toot and grunted its way out of the station toward Valencia.

The trip took almost seven hours and ranks as a milestone in our experience. I think everyone should go to Spain, if for no other reason than to ride on a third-class train. It is a singular event in the evolution of transportation that will some day be only a memory. When the Spanish railways increase their freight-handling capabilities and make it obsolete, you'll have to go to India for the same sensation.

It took almost an hour to retrieve our bikes, buy tickets for San Roque (the nearest Spanish station to Gibraltar), recheck our bikes with the next baggage department, and finally get out of the station into the clear night and bright lights of downtown Valencia.

Using two phrases from our Spanish phrase book, "Tenemos mucha hambre" (we are very hungry) and "no mucho dinero" (not much money), we flagged down the first policeman we saw.

He looked at our unshaven faces, then down at our dirty sweaters, jeans and ragged tennis shoes, then back up and nodded in understanding, with a big smile. Motioning for us to follow him, he led us through the busy streets, past several cafés and into a narrow lane where he drew us up at a small, clean, crowded café.

"Aqui no mucho dinero," he smiled and hurried off the way we'd come.

The food was good, the people pleasant, and best of all, the price there was almost half the food prices at places near the station. When in doubt, ask a cop. If they don't know personally, they know someone who does, and they rarely lead you astray. *In a civilized country, the most omniscient person in any given neighborhood is the cop working the street.* It was a lesson we learned early in our traveling and never forgot.

We were back at the depot early to board our train, where we would be riding for the night. It was different from the one we'd come in on from Vinaroz in that it had padding on the benches and doors on the compartments. Since we were among the first passengers aboard, we found an empty compartment easily, thinking that, since it was late, perhaps we'd have it to ourselves and could sleep the night. At 10:48, the train crept out of the station, and our compartment was still empty. Aha! Good bit of luck. Good night, amigos.

But 15 minutes later the train ground to a halt, heralding a rush of passengers from the suburban station, three of whom pushed loudly into our compartment. Much disgruntled, we sat up and made space, unable to stretch out our legs any more.

The train had just started moving again, it seemed, when again it stopped to allow another rush of Spaniards to storm aboard, three more in our compartment. This continued, despite our threats and protests, until there were 12 of us, packed shoulder to shoulder. The space between the benches was so limited that we sat with knees overlapping alternatively.

"I haven't even got enough room to scratch," said Bob. "Do you think any of them are going to get off in the night?"

"It won't make much difference if they do," I said. "Just look at that corridor."

The passageway outside was already filling up with Spaniards unable to find places to sit, and it was going to get worse before it got better.

"We're lucky to have a place at all," muttered Geoff. "But it's going to be a long night."

The other passengers accepted the conditions naturally, half of them already on their way to sleep. Soon we were all dozing in the muggy compartment, to the symphony of typewriter-like clacking coming from the rails below.

When one of us would get up in the night, to struggle down the crowded corridor to the foul-smelling cubicle at the end of the car, he would have to warn the other two before he left. Then they would stand guard, firmly, to halt the rush for the vacant seat, thereby initiating a lot of vigorous argument, they babbling in Spanish and we in English, until the third returned and regained his place.

It soon became extremely hot and stuffy in the airless compartment, the window tightly shut and the corridor full of smoke and sweat from the press of bodies. The air became so thick we could almost chew it before choking it down. Slowly the hours passed as the train chugged its way overland toward the high country around

Cordoba, with us sitting slumped and swaying with the rocking motion throughout the night.

All the next day we rode across Spain, changing trains three times, traveling with two English girls part of the way, ending up that night in a whistle stop called Rodriquez. The next train heading our direction wasn't leaving until late the following morning.

You only learn what really works by trying things that don't work. Keep questioning, evaluating. Ask, "Could there be a better way?" Sometimes what you need is a break, a chance to stop, to stand back, to reconsider.

Again, we retrieved our bicycles, began our endless quest for food and then pedaled out of town to camp on the outskirts.

The next morning, we rode in from the eucalyptus grove where we'd slept the night in time to catch the southbound cattle car to El Golea, where once more we had to change. The platform superintendent in El Golea informed us that our tickets would have to be changed for second class, at an additional charge, if we didn't want to wait until the next afternoon for the third-class train, which we didn't.

The conductor of the second-class train refused to have our bicycles in his baggage car, saying that they must go on the third-class train the following day. His reasons for this, we soon gathered, were that bicycles were a trifle demeaning for a man of his status to deal with.

But after 15 minutes of heated argument, the bicycles were loaded into the small baggage car, and we continued on our way. I felt sure that this would be the silliest incident I would ever be involved with in dealings with public officials. In retrospect, it doesn't even receive honorable mention.

The second-class train consisted of only one self-contained car, with the engine in the forward section and baggage compartment in the rear, the padded passenger section occupying the center three-quarters of the car.

San Roque was two hours down the line, two comfortable hours in the modern airy coach, made more enjoyable by comparison with what we had experienced for the past 48 hours. We sat across from two American women who had flown from Vancouver to Madrid two days before, which set us thinking of our departure in the rain seven months back. We'd come a long way, we felt, in these months, by car, foot, thumb, bicycle and now train—not to mention 2,000 miles by ship and a few by ferry. And yet we were only two flying days away from home on a little train in Spain. *It's amazing what you can do with a little money—and what you must do when you have very little money to accomplish the same end.* But there are things that money can't buy. Some things have to be paid for in a different type of currency—things, for instance, like memories.

As we clamored out of our seats upon our arrival in San Roque, grabbing our rucksacks from the overhead shelves, Bob's machete slid out of its sheath and dropped onto the man below. The man bellowed in pain, holding up his hand dripping with blood from a two-inch cut. Three or four passengers hurried forward excitedly, as Bob stood helplessly, holding the retrieved machete.

"Get out the first aid kit, Bob. It's in your pack, isn't it?"

I gave the distressed, bleeding Spaniard a confident smile, and clapped his handkerchief from his breast pocket over the cut, then led him to the door of the car. Geoff had joined Bob on the platform, and the sketchy bundle of bandages and antiseptic was ready to be used in seconds.

With an efficiency that would have gladdened the heart of our first aid instructor, we cleaned, dressed, bandaged, and taped the shallow cut tight under a roll of white gauze strips. With a final pat, we boosted the confused gentleman back into the car just as it started moving, closing the door behind him; and we smiled professionally until the little train was out of sight.

A crowd of 20 people had gathered to view this scene, standing back about 10 feet, silently, as if to "give the patient room to breath." We had the definite feeling that that sort of thing wasn't done too often in San Roque.

Bob refastened his pack and slipped it on, joining us where we waited with the bicycles. The last eight kilometers to Gibraltar were over a dusty farm road that wound through a range of low hills before becoming paved and descending to the border post of La Linea and "The Rock," the end of the first leg of our trip to Johannesburg.

THE PURPOSE OF PAIN

Nature sends us pain of all kinds—physical, emotional, and financial—to tell us to stop doing certain things. I suggest that you become an "inverse paranoid," a person who is convinced that a great conspiracy exists—and it is aimed at making you successful and happy!

Whenever God wants to send you a gift, he wraps it up in a problem. The bigger the gift, the bigger the problem it comes wrapped up in. Nature also sends you peace, pleasure and happiness to tell you what you should do more of. So, look into your greatest difficulty for the gift that it contains. It's always there.

CHAPTER 10

GIBRALTAR DAYS

A person rarely has the chance to witness such deliberate, childish, stupid, and yet official pigheadedness as that which we experienced for three hours at the Spanish border post leading into Gibraltar.

Spain's government, in the wake of receding British influence, was making a determined effort to establish a claim to the Rock and force the British to give it up. One of their schemes in the plan of protracted aggravation was the limiting of tourist traffic across the border into the colony, accomplished by insisting on hold-ups and searches that lasted for hours.

If the Spanish police had taken lessons, they couldn't have been more irritating. One American family in front of us had to wait for three hours, then unload their station wagon completely onto tables for inspection. Without even looking, the police ordered everything re-packed into the car, only to come out in half an hour to demand it all be unloaded again. We arrived at 2 p.m. when the family had already been there for four hours, and they passed into Gibraltar just ahead of us at 5 p.m. How a government could resort to that form of pettiness was beyond our limited comprehension.

On the other side of the customs bay, hundreds of Spanish workers entered and departed in a steady stream, with no questions asked. We waited in line for three hours, patiently, before they condescended to put a chalk mark on our unopened packs and allow us through.

The blue-uniformed British officials, one kilometer further, simply assured themselves that we were not potential welfare cases, and then stamped us through. It left me with definite opinions concerning who should control the colony.

It was April 20, and we had achieved our objective, Gibraltar, from London, in 17 days, at a cost of $460. Our remaining assets consisted of $540, three very worn bicycles, three rucksacks, and about $20 worth of camping gear, not including our sleeping bags or clothes. And we could see Africa looming out of the haze on the Moroccan coast, just 20 miles away across the straits. We had completed the third stage in our journey.

"Hey! Brother world-beaters! The water's great! Come on, you can't sleep forever!"

I was back from an early swim in the crystal-blue water lapping the beach in Sandy Cove, our new home. Geoff and Bob were buried in their bags, and I could have been talking to myself for all the reaction I was getting.

At last a voice mumbled out of the depths of one of the misshapen quilted lumps on the sand.

"Geoff? Geoff, buddy?"

"Yeah?" came the guarded reply.

"Do you hear anything, Geoff?"

"Yeah. I hate to admit it, but I think I do."

"What is it? What does it sound like?"

"I think someone's strangling a cat."

"Well, tell them to go down the beach and strangle it. About a half mile down the beach!"

At that, I grabbed the two sleeping bags and hefted them up, dumping their occupants onto the warm sand, blinking at the morning sunshine.

"Let's drown him," growled Bob.

"Let's castrate him first, then drown him," said Geoff.

We splashed and dove, yelling gleefully in the crisp salt water, teaming up and jumping on the odd man, then jumping on the teammate and being dunked in return. For 10 minutes we cavorted in the tingling surf before dragging ashore and making our way back to the sleeping bags.

Drying off in the warm morning sun, we discussed our next move, as we had done the evening before, after being directed to this beach and making camp. The situation was altered beyond recognition from our tentative planning in Vancouver and London. All our thinking had to be considerably revised.

There was no question about the bicycles. They had to go, and the sooner the better. We could barely stand to look at them, as they had caused us so much heartache and strain—strain we could still feel in our legs after almost three weeks.

We had to get back onto four wheels. We realized now that it had been foolish to start out on bicycles in the first place, and it would be doubly foolish to continue with them now. We needed a vehicle.

In search of a Land Rover

We had arrived in Gibraltar with 180 pounds, full of ambition and ideals, with no idea of what was ahead in Africa. We were yet to see a reliable map of the continent, and beyond Algeria and Morocco, we had very little idea of the geography.

On the one-page map in our atlas, the Sahara Desert and the tropical belt were indicated by yellow and green colors. Strewn through this area were several countries, which we would cross when we came to them. Nothing to worry about, we thought. That brought us back to the vehicle; what would it be?

A Land Rover was the first answer. What little reading we had done about overland traveling, we noted the name "Land Rover" in almost every article. We considered buying one once while we were still in Vancouver, but wrote it off as being too expensive for our limited budget. Now we found that we couldn't afford not to have one. We hid our gear in the rocks at one end of the little beach and set out to take care of first things first—securing a Land Rover.

We knew there were Land Rovers in Gibraltar, but we didn't know where, so we flagged down the first one we saw and asked the driver. The Land Rovers in Gibraltar were mostly military vehicles, we were told, except those bought by civilians at auctions for private use. The last army auction had been five weeks before, and the next one wouldn't be until July; we would have to find one for sale by a civilian. We rode into the town to find a policeman.

Always ask a cop—you can't go wrong. The first bobby we spoke to gave us the name and address of a man who had sold his Land Rover the week before. He gave us a few pointers for buying a vehicle, and referred us to another man, a Mr. Earnest Harten, at the Roots Group Garage.

Mr. Harten was a thin, balding fellow with that confident attitude of people who deal in used cars—that attitude which seems to say, "Whether you buy it or not makes little difference to me, but you'll never find a better deal." However, his friendly attitude dispelled many of the doubts we had about buying a used car in a foreign country (colony).

He listened to our requirements and our heart-rending story and then assured us that he might know someone with a Land Rover for sale. He told us to return that afternoon.

In the next three hours we looked at two light trucks, a couple of cars, and two Land Rovers, one almost new priced at 300 pounds, and the other almost ready for the scrap heap, at 90 pounds.

We had never bought a Land Rover before, but we were far from babes when it came to buying used cars. Between Geoff and me, we'd bought, driven, and ruined about eight cars. We had one rule which we relied on: if the body is good, the running gear will also be good, and vice versa. Simple, but true, and we'd never gone wrong with it.

When we returned that afternoon, Mr. Harten greeted us with a smile and led us to the vehicle. It was not impressive—windows dirty, canvas top, paint flaking off. We walked around it critically.

"Does it run?"

"I'll start it up, if you like. There we go. How's that?"

"Sounds all right."

We went over it from one end to the other, checking the water, oil, and undercarriage, and then took it for a drive. The steering was good, and the brakes caught readily enough. The only complaint was the clutch. Mr. Harten assured us that the clutch would last another 5,000 miles.

We then took the Land Rover for a short test drive, parked it in the same place, and walked back to Root's Garage with Mr. Harten. He wanted 120 pounds, nothing less. We told him we'd let him know within a day or two.

"Now we are in a fix," said Bob. "If we buy the Rover and insure it, we'll be too broke to go anywhere in it."

Immersed in thought, we rode back to our camp on the beach, each of us trying to think of a solution. It was a strange problem, in that we were not broke, and yet we had run out of money. We'd come too far to go back, yet we couldn't go on. Behind us was Europe and before us was Africa, but all we could see was Africa. One solution was right at hand, though, and we discussed it briefly.

I learned later that *the hallmark of all successful people is that they are intensely solution-oriented and future-oriented. They constantly ask "How?" in relation to their goals in order to solve their problems. They think in terms of where they're going rather than where they've been.*

We could sell our bicycles, load everything on our backs, and set off hitchhiking. With the money we had, we could get back to England or start into Africa. "But let's be honest," we said. "We started out to achieve something, and we aren't going to achieve anything by becoming bums who wave their thumbs as if the world owes us a ride." In our travels, we had met many bums, often with more money than the people from whom they were begging rides and accepting free meals.

We had met fellows who bragged about having $500 in travelers checks in their pockets and $3,000 in banks at home, but they were saving on transportation so they would have more money to spend on liquor and entertainment when they arrived in the big cities. We felt there was a hole in any reasoning that went against *the principle of a person's responsibility to pay his or her own way.* Naturally, there are occasionally extenuating circumstances that cast one on the whims of fate, but these are backward steps, which have to be made up before one is even again. *No one has the right to base his or her actions solely on charity, to begin a course of action on the assumption that someone else will foot the bill, or the opposite, not to undertake a thing just because there is no one to stand as a backstop.*

One reason we had decided on bicycles in London was that they would give us a certain independence, a sort of freedom to ourselves not enjoyed by those who feel that they have no need to provide their own transportation. We had not traveled like kings, but neither had we expected to travel first class. At least we were three independent beings, taking nothing from the country we traveled through and asking nothing. We weren't rich, but we weren't slaves to the unpredictability of the oncoming traffic either. Although going back was a grim alternative, hitchhiking, except in an emergency or in desperation, was one shade worse.

The desire or attempt to get something for nothing in any area of life is destructive to the soul and spirit of an individual. The decision to pay one's own way on the other hand, to pay in full, braces the personality and strengthens the character. *Self-reliance is a source of pride and self-respect. Trying to live off of others is a source of shame.*

Our pressing need was for money, for a cold cash injection that would put the trip to Africa back on its feet. The question was, where and how were we going to come by this elixir of life? The work force in Gibraltar consisted of Spaniards earning an average of $15 per week. Since we ate more than that each week, we quickly ruled out the idea of taking jobs. We would either have to borrow the money, or give up altogether.

Borrowing. The word leaves a bad taste in the mouths of self-reliant people. It denotes debt and bankruptcy and repossessed television sets, ruined friendships, and ne'er-do-wells. But on the other hand, it is the foundation stone of the western world, upon which our lives were built. It is the credit system that allows pleasure and necessity to be dealt with immediately, and repaid when possible. I had bought my cars and insurance, as had Geoff, on this system. We had received our education under the secure wing of borrowed capital. We had bought clothes and spare parts, rented homes and apartments, pulled our friends out of difficulties with pregnant girlfriends, financed chums in buying cars and paying rent—all on credit. For years we had been both recipients and benefactors of the borrowing system, and one thing we could honestly say: We had never left a debt unpaid.

We had been in debt before and would again, and felt no shame toward borrowing or borrowers, secure as we were in ourselves and our ability, not only to repay but also to accept repaying as a moral obligation, irrevocable, and not to be shirked because of distance or the passing of time. We felt that, having always borrowed and always repaid, we had earned the right to do it again when the occasion arose. And the occasion had arisen.

For the remainder of the afternoon, we sat on a beach and wrote letters to friends, explaining our position clearly and asking for loans, to be repaid when we reached Johannesburg and began working again. Most of the letters were addressed to people from whom we had extracted vows to call on them if we ever ran short and needed financial assistance. So we wrote: "Well, faithful friends, this is the pinch. You can't come with us personally on this journey, but you can accompany us in spirit; you will be sharing the adventure by helping to make it possible." Just before the post office closed that evening, we sent all letters air express, plus two telegrams. Then we could do nothing but wait.

A SURPRISE ANNOUNCEMENT

That evening on the beach, much to our surprise, Bob announced that he was cashing in his chips. He had enough of sweating and insecurity and was fed up. He said that he would rather go back to England than sit like a fool on a lonely beach waiting for money to come so he could go out and risk his life some more.

"You can't be serious, Bob. Not after all we've been through together?"

"Come on, Bob. What good are two musketeers? How can you leave us when Africa is within our grasp? Look! You can almost touch the lights of Morocco."

"I'm not sold on this idea anymore. Why don't we give it up and go to the beaches in Southern France? That we can do with the money we have left."

"But Bob, we've come all this way to go to Africa. We can't just quit!"

"Think about it, Bob. Don't make up your mind tonight. It's late; and it's been a long day. We'll talk about it in the morning, what do you say?"

"I don't need to think about it anymore," he said. "I've been thinking about it since Barcelona, and I've made up my mind. One third of the money is mine, and tomorrow I'll take my share and leave."

We tried to argue, using our long friendship as a lever, but it was no use. He had locked onto the idea of going back to England or France, like a bulldog, and staunchly refused to budge. We dropped the subject and turned in for the night.

Our hope for a change of heart failed to materialize. The next morning, after hiding our gear in the rocks, we rode back to the Barclays Bank in town and cashed the travelers checks. Glumly, Geoff and I paid him 60 pounds, and Bob went off to sell his bicycle, leaving Geoff and me alone at the bank.

"What do we do from here?"

"I think we should buy the Land Rover and find a way to continue to Africa now."

"I can't envision going back. After all this, it would be ridiculous."

"Let's go and see if Harten will accept 100 pounds for the Rover."

To our surprise, Mr. Harten accepted the offer, and we took delivery of the Rover that afternoon. We drove back toward Sandy Cove, our beach, to test the four-wheel drive in the sand. Coming around one of the sharp corners on the sea cliff road, we almost ran over Bob. He was riding into town to deliver his bicycle to a shop and move into a youth hostel at the far end of the main street.

Having no hard feelings, Geoff and I offered Bob a lift in *our* Land Rover, which he sheepishly accepted. Moments later he sheepishly asked us if we had any openings for a spare driver to Africa.

"I didn't think you'd buy the Rover," said Bob. "I thought you'd give it up without the money, and then we would all go back together."

"Bob, old buddy, we are never going to give it up. Not now, not if the money runs out, not ever—until we get to Johannesburg."

"Anyway, welcome back. We're glad to have you aboard again."

I learned that *all great achievements begin with a leap of faith, an irrevocable commitment, a burning of the boats. Act boldly and unseen forces will come to your aid.*

That afternoon we drove up and down the sandy beach, tires churning, engine roaring, and three light-headed world-beaters cheering wildly. After supper, cooked beside the vehicle on the sand, we drove into Gibraltar and got drunk for the first time in a month. The lights on the Moroccan coast seemed 10 miles closer.

Strange how our perceptions are so colored by the news of the day. What only moments earlier seems remote and distant and difficult with one positive note now seems doable, close, and even imminent.

THE ROCK OF GIBRALTAR

Shaped like a disfigured pear, cut off by a narrow channel and connected by a two-lane causeway, Gibraltar extends from the mainland like a small Anglo-Saxon island on the edge of a Spanish sea. The famous rock fills the easterly two-thirds, the city of Gibraltar draped compactly on the western base, flowing down to the harbor. On the eastern side, at the bottom of the steep rain catcher, the narrow winding road from the city that snakes around the cliffs ends at a sheer stone face just above the tiny beach where we had set up camp. High above the road, the solid rock looms at an angle of 70 degrees, to an altitude of 2,200 feet, almost like a cliff, cutting off the sun to the beach below at 3 p.m. every day. But the beach was largely deserted, except on the weekends, and there we made our temporary home.

We reckoned that it would take six days to receive replies to our requests for additional finances, and we set about filling the hours as constructively as possible, sure that the money would come, and wanting to be prepared for departure when it did.

The day following Bob's defection and subsequent return was Sunday. The beach began filling with tourists and Gibraltarians shortly after 9 a.m. Our haphazard procedure of tossing the sleeping bags on the beach each night to sleep, and then tossing them back among the rocks each day, was senseless if we were to be staying there for six days or more. So, choosing the most ideal spot against the sea wall running the length of the little beach, we labored all day in the hot sun, carrying rocks from the base of the cliff to build walls, giving us a little protection from the breezes that came up every day or two, as well as some privacy. We completed a three-walled enclosure about four feet high, open to the sky and roomy enough for us to cook and move around inside.

We mutually gave up smoking and started training a little, throwing our football back and forth, or running out for passes into the water, shouting and splashing. The water was crystal clear and cool, shimmering in the bright sun that shined all the days we spent in the tiny colony. We swam every morning, increasing the distance daily until we reached a mile. Our skin began to take on a copper tan, light at first, then darker as we spent hours in the warmth of the Mediterranean early summer. Slowly the days passed with no reply from our friends.

The Land Rover was put into the garage for two days to have the muffler repaired and the electrical system checked, the spark plugs changed, and the contacts cleaned. At the same time, we bought five, five-gallon jerry cans, two for water and three for gasoline, and a small tool kit, to add to the spare parts that we had ordered from the Roots Garage. With a little black-and-gold enamel, the Bon Vivant emblem was proudly painted on both doors, adding the finishing touch to the vehicle.

Every day we inquired at the post office, the telegraph office, and the bank to see if there had been any replies. "Not today, boys," or "Nothing yet", or "Maybe later on, call this afternoon," the answers came back.

We had photographs taken and then driving tests for our International Driving Permits, as well as our Gibraltar licenses. The health center in the main square informed us that we needed yellow fever vaccinations, on top of boosters for Typhus A and Tetanus. We signed the forms and paid one pound each. We then laid awake the entire night, moaning at the paralyzed numbness in our left arms and shoulders. Geoff had a tooth filled at a small clinic in town, while Bob and I took the remaining bicycles to the large shop inside the city gates and sold them, for one-third of the original price. We were glad to be rid of them.

And every day, morning and evening, we pilgrimaged to the communications offices to check for the replies that never came.

At night, we parked the Rover and roamed the streets in search of bars with jukeboxes carrying tunes we wanted to hear again, before we said good-bye to civilization. We became regular customers of several places, dropping in each evening for a glass of beer and a little chat about our impending trip. The Dollar Bar, run by old Ben and his two married daughters, became our favorite hangout, a hole-in-the-wall place, but comfortable and always cheery. "Behold a Pale Horse" starring Gregory Peck was showing at the main theater in town. We'd all seen it, but we went again, attending the movies at the military theater, and the small show house in the old part of town, on other quiet nights. Still the days passed slowly, and there was nothing for us at the post office.

Waiting can be the hardest type of work, because you see no progress and find no relief from anxiety.

The sun rose at 5 a.m., becoming so warm by 6 a.m. that we would have to abandon our sleeping bags from the perspiration. The first thing we saw in the morning was the green Land Rover with its black-and-gold emblem, standing patiently by our open "house," as if to reproach us for failing to take it to Africa, as we had promised. Once into town, the streets were alive with colorful clothing shops, run by ivory-toothed, smiling Hindus, always good for a bartering session on our way to the post office and the bank.

There were flowers everywhere in Gibraltar during those thrilling spring days, filling the windows and store fronts, overflowing from the carts pushed by the shawled Spanish women along the narrow main street. Music leaped at us from the wide doorways of the many modern stores selling duty-free radios and tape recorders, gifts and souvenirs. Daily, we trudged hopefully to the post office and resignedly to the bank, pessimistically to the telegraph office, and then deflatedly back to the Rover and home to the beach.

If the shadow of defeat had not hovered over us, we could have enjoyed those days in Gibraltar immensely. The weather was consistently beautiful, the people warm and friendly, the living cheap, and the pace of life soft and easy. But always the grim specter of failure rose to taunt us, to make a mockery of our fading nonchalance. The hardest part wasn't the waiting; we could wait for anything and for as long as necessary. The hard thing was simply not knowing, the silence from the outside world that was neither a negation of our requests, nor an affirmation.

We had worked it out in our minds so neatly, and written so eloquently, that it didn't seem possible our letters could be ignored. What was holding up the replies, and more important, the money? Sitting there on the beach by our Land Rover, ready to go, we felt like brides at the church with no groom in sight.

On the ninth day after mailing the letters, we received a reply from my Aunt Barbara. I had asked her for 100 pounds, if she could spare it, and a certain suitcase from her garage, which she could send air freight.

The reply was ripped open eagerly, with trembling fingers:

> *"Dear Brian, I have forwarded your suitcase as you
> requested. You owe me six pounds, which I suppose I'll never
> see. As for your request for money, if you think I can afford to
> finance your aimless wanderings while you squander your
> youth to no good purpose, you will have to think again. You
> had no right going off without enough money to pay for your
> entire trip, and I am not prepared to rectify your mistakes.
> Why don't you boys take a job in Gibraltar and work for six
> months? You don't really care how you waste your time."*

The letter continued another page and a half, ending with a mention of how nicely her geraniums were blooming this spring.

So that was it. That was what they thought about our great adventure. That was why there had been no replies, no money, no response at all. Glumly, we drove back to the beach and parked, sitting in the Rover in silence. Everything had been so perfect, we thought. All the details were wrapped up and taken care of. We had found a seed called Africa, planted it, and nurtured it until it grew and bore fruit in our minds. But now we lacked the financial resources to reap the harvest, while the sun beat down and the fruit rotted on the branch.

How foolish we must look! Three boys playing a silly game called, "Let's be men and go to Africa." Three improvident youths living in a cheap utopia made of high ideals and childish fantasies—that's what we were to everyone else, and we were the only ones too dense to see it. Even a little old lady could see into our senseless dream world and hold the reality up for us to cringe before, like catching us with a stolen cookie, shame-faced and tongue-tied. After all our hopes and plans, our glorious ambitions, our eagerness to do battle with life in the dark continent, this is what it comes down to—a triumvirate of worthless juveniles, tilting at windmills?

We wondered if they all felt that way, that this trip, so precious to us, was just a useless waste of time. That night, we dejectedly discussed possibilities of driving back to England and starting over. We could sell our watches, if need be, for petrol, and perhaps try again in five months or so. We'd made our big try and lost, and we could not stay in Gibraltar forever. Perhaps it would be better if we did something a little more "realistic."

We didn't go into town that night. Instead we sat on the dark beach beside our Land Rover, gazing out at the empty sea. We felt like old men on a lonely shore, unneeded and unappreciated by an indifferent world. The lights of Morocco now seemed very faint, and very far away.

THE OPINIONS OF OTHERS

Don't let your dreams be destroyed by the opinions of other people, including close relatives. You alone know what the goal means to you; other people have a different perspective. They may be well-meaning in their criticism, but they simply don't understand. Out of respect, you might listen to their words and weigh them, but the decision—and its consequences—are yours alone to bear.

CHAPTER 11

THE TURNING POINT

The next day was Sunday, and "our beach" was half full of relaxed Gibraltarians, strolling along the water's edge or picnicking in the bright sunshine. With the happy laughter and tinkling music around us, we tossed off our shroud of discouragement somewhat, swimming and tossing the ball around energetically. If we couldn't go to Africa, that didn't mean we had to cry about it. There was always tomorrow, and tomorrow we could come back to Gibraltar and try again. No matter what, we would keep the Land Rover and the tools intact, for the next try, in a few months time. Disappointed? Yes. But defeated? Never!

Africa would still be there in September, and this time we wouldn't make any mistakes. We had fought and lost; but the first battle didn't decide the war. We were saddened all right, but we weren't destroyed. It was a shame that we had come so far, only to be turned back on the very threshold, but we were only down, not out, by a long shot.

On Monday morning, staunch as Vikings, we strode to the post office, determined to accept the worst and carry on from there. Smiling bravely, we presented ourselves at Poste Restaunte, like disciplined soldiers walking before a firing squad. There was one thin letter waiting for Geoff, from a friend of his father in London, whom Geoff had met only once in his childhood, and to whom he had written requesting 75 pounds, humbly explaining the position. We waited patiently, like doomed men, hearing the rifles cocked as the letter was quickly torn open.

Geoff read it to himself, then aloud to us, and suddenly the world burst into a blaze of light and music, a joyous, crashing symphony of glorious relief and reprieve. The siege was lifted; the cavalry had come thundering to the rescue. We were world-beaters again in a burst of exultation and triumph. Slapping each other on the back, laughing riotously and jumping up and down in excitement, we made him read it again. It was brief and to the point:

> Dear Geoffrey,
> Your father wrote and told me you would be in London
> sometime this winter, and I look forward to seeing you again as

a grown man. However, it will wait until you return from your journey into Africa. It is unfortunate that you have exhausted your finances, but as I was once a young man in similar circumstances, I appreciate how easy it is to under-budget, much more when you have so little idea of what to budget for. It is a wonderful thing you boys have embarked upon; it would be a shame to abandon it for the sake of an innocent miscalculation of expenses. You must employ your youth to the full while you have the opportunity, and before you become burdened with responsibilities. To assure that you experience no further difficulties, I have ordered my bank to transfer the sum of 150 pounds to you, care of Barclays Bank, Gibraltar. Please do not feel that you are under any pressure for repayment, and if there is anything further I can do for you, please do not hesitate to write. Please extend my regards to your two friends, and may I wish you all, Good Traveling.
    —Yours faithfully, Jack S. Turing

How can a person express gratitude so great it wells up in the throat like a shower full of tears? And to a man we had never met, in a distant city, who had, in a kindly gesture of warmth and encouragement, changed our whole lives? We had come to our Rubicon at the Gates of Hercules, and a hand had reached across the miles, pushing us confidently into the current. It was not a question of whether we would succeed, or whether it was advisable. It was the simple realization that we must have the chance, and by giving it to us, to do with as we could according to our abilities, Mr. Jack S. Turing became our inspirational symbol, the banner under which we proudly entered into Africa.

This was a most important lesson. *If you make a total commitment to a goal and you hang on long enough, something always happens.* Many people lose heart and give up just one day, one step, one action before the breakthrough that leads to great success. *It is as if nature poses a test to see how badly you really want it, and at that moment you demonstrate what you're really made of.*

ONE THIN LETTER

What a difference a letter can make! One letter of rejection can dash your hopes and call into question your very purpose. It paints you as a vain and foolish vagabond. One letter of acceptance then restores your faith, validates your mission, and ultimately makes the remainder of your journey possible. The special irony is that the affirmation or assistance may come from a distant relative—or even a total stranger.

SECTION 4:
THE DAWN OF REALITY

Most great success in life comes just one step beyond where you are ready to quit. There is a time in your life when you feel yourself suddenly beyond caring, completely willing to accept the outcome, whatever it is. And at that moment, fate intervenes. Destiny acts. Something happens.

Every test you take and pass on your journey merely prepares you for more difficult tests and challenges. They never end. They only change and become tougher as you grow and mature.

Never wish for things to be easier. Instead, wish that you were stronger and better. Never seek the easy way out. Instead look for the hard way through.

Nature is kind. She never sends you a problem that is too big for you to handle. She is clever as well. She prepares you step by step, raising the bar, the requirements, gradually, until you are ready for the big tests when they come.

As long as you have a clear goal and a plan, and you are willing to be flexible in the face of changing circumstances, you will continue to move onward and upward.

You will eventually look back and be amazed at how far you have come. But it is nothing in comparison to how far you have yet to go.

CHAPTER 12

MOROCCO AND THE ATLAS MOUNTAINS

On Thursday, May 4 at 2 p.m., we drove off the ferry in Tangiers, continuing, after a brief customs formality, into the city, the now topless Land Rover heavily laden with cans, boxes of tinned food, the well-packed equipment and clothes, and on top, with Bob, two English girls who were only riding with us as far as Tangiers. We seemed to have just about everything.

The food took up most of the space in the back, making the Rover look like an overland delivery wagon. Calculating the distance, we anticipated being on the road for 30 days to Lagos, Nigeria, our next objective. Thus, the food buying was simplified immensely. We just bought 30 cans of each item—of beans, spaghetti, meatballs, sausage, peaches, and green peas. We had 48 cans of condensed milk to go with the tea and coffee, plus bullion cubes and sugar, salt, pepper, and garlic. The total cost, including two petrol burners for cooking, came to just under $100.

We reckoned that two meals per day would be sufficient, morning and evening, and the monotony of diet threatened by the lack of variety would be offset by the time lapse between the two meals, assuring hunger enough to make anything welcome. Somehow, we managed to be wrong in almost every calculation we made, until it seemed safer in the long run to work it out and then to do the closest to the opposite we could find. But, in the process of planning on a two-meal daily diet, we had been quite correct. We could always supplement it with tea or bullion cubes.

MY KINGDOM FOR A MAP

At a large, Spanish-type house overlooking the sea on the outskirts of the city, we dropped off the two girls, wishing them luck in their proposed plans to work the summer in an orphanage. We returned to the Casbah, the main shopping area, to buy insurance for the vehicle, not having done so in Gibraltar.

At this point, we felt we should finally get a map for the coming journey. After a couple of hours of searching, we were surprised and chagrined to find that there were no maps of Africa and the Sahara Desert available in Tangiers.

We knew that a map, at this point, was essential. We tried the Michelin Tire Company offices and asked if they had a map of Africa. The receptionist had no idea and went back to speak to her boss, a Monsieur Tourneau.

Monsieur Tourneau politely informed us that Michelin did not sell maps, only tires. We thanked him politely and went back to the car. As we sat there mulling over our situation, he suddenly appeared, looked at us searchingly, and then handed us a map and walked away.

I still remember that time and place, in the warm afternoon in the parking lot. We somehow felt that this was an important moment. We opened the map, fully two feet by three feet, and gazed at a miracle of the modern world.

It was Michelin map number 163, covering Africa from the Mediterranean across Morocco, Algeria, and south almost 3,000 miles. It was incredible, detailing every city, town, and landmark across the Sahara and into sub-Saharan Africa. It had obviously been made over many years, when the French governed much of Africa. In the weeks ahead, it turned out to be an incredible blessing. I cannot imagine how we could have survived without it. It definitely saved our lives.

I later learned that usually *any map or plan is better than none; and if it is complete enough, as this map was, it can make the critical difference between victory and defeat.* It is amazing how many otherwise talented and intelligent people underachieve and fail in life because of poor or nonexistent preparation. Sometimes the first 10 percent of the time you invest in doing your homework turns out to contain 90 percent of the value of the entire process.

Two hours and $48 later, insured for the entirety of the continent for three months, we were traveling on the southbound road for Rabat, singing, "It won't be long, no, it won't be long."

Send Rover Right Over

We had been right; it wasn't long. It was a short 12 kilometers out of Tangiers when we started learning interesting things about our beloved Land Rover. We learned, for instance, that the radiator was no good. In fact, it was bubbling, boiling, steaming, and pouring water all over the road.

A couple of minutes of stupidly staring at the radiator assured us that it would not be a bad idea for us to sit and wait for it to cool, which we did. We had no chance to drive for any distance in the confines of Gibraltar's limited roads, and breaking down so quickly on the open road did not present itself as a good omen.

"Cripes! Look at the steam! The bloody radiator looks ruined. Haven't we got enough troubles?"

"Apparently not."

"Are you trying to be funny?"

"Nope."

"Did you fill the water jerry cans, Bob?"

"What do you mean, did I fill them? That was your job, wasn't it?"

"Yeah? Who says it was my job?"

"Oh, shut up, both of you. I filled them."

Driving with two wheels on the gravel shoulder to keep out of the way of passing traffic, we slowly drove the 12 kilometers back to town to find a repair shop.

"I wonder how much it's going to cost?"

"Probably a king's ransom."

"Yeah, these Arabs are notorious thieves."

"And con men."

"And swindlers."

"Can't we go a little bit faster?"

"Why?"

"Oh, I'm just getting a little tired of kids on bicycles going by us and laughing."

"Well then, I've got just the answer."

"Yeah, what?"

"Don't look at them."

At the first dusty little workshop we came to on the outskirts of town, we turned in and armed ourselves with the French dictionary before getting out. With exaggerated expressions of woe, thumbing frantically through the little book, we outlined our misfortunes to the sweat-stained, T-shirted proprietor of "Alphonso's." We finally had to lead him to the vehicle and point out the felonious radiator, at which he brightened knowledgeably.

Nodding and smiling like a door-to-door salesman, Alphonso regretted that he couldn't help us personally, but if we would go with him into town, he would take us to his friend, who was in the radiator business. Dubiously, we fell in behind the battered pick-up and followed him through the streets.

"Where are we going?"

"He's taking us to a friend of his."

"What for?"

"Probably to share the pickings. You know, one fellow directs the suckers to the other, and afterwards, they divide the loot between them."

He stopped in front of a tiny shop with the word "RADIA-TORS" over the door, and jovially introduced us to his worried friend, Manuel (Who's that? His partner in crime, I guess). After the customary round of hand shaking, they jabbered together in Arabic for a few seconds. (What's that they're saying? They're deciding how much they can take us for? What do you think?) Our misgivings were rising by the moment.

We were hoping for a quick, and inexpensive, repair job, perhaps a few seconds with an acetylene torch, and then we would be on our way. But then again, we had had problems in the past with radiators, ruined radiators that had to be replaced, and this one, in light of our experience, appeared well beyond repair.

Alphonso left us in the hands of his partner in crime and disappeared with an uninspiring "Bon voyage!" Manuel said the radiator would have to come out, and when we had complied with the request, he proceeded to strip it down with astounding proficiency, demonstrating to us, beyond doubt, that the radiator was indeed irreparable.

Stoically, we resigned ourselves to fate and the procuring of another radiator, a job that included a tour of three scrap yards and the careful, critical inspection of five used radiators. After having examined the fourth and rejecting it, Manuel ceased to be looked upon as a Barbary pirate and was accorded instead the respect due a conscientious craftsman. Our fears about being bilked turned out to be groundless. Manuel, finally satisfied with the fifth radiator, haggled the price down to half that originally demanded when the greasy Arab in the scrap yard perceived that it was for tourists that the article was being purchased.

After four hours of searching, testing, welding, and checking for further defects, the bill came to $17, and the radiator, now reinstalled in the Rover, was functioning perfectly. We gave him $20 and much thanks, the part alone having cost $13. That sort of sincere honesty, we felt, had to be encouraged.

One of the wonderful things you learn in life is that *most people you meet are good, honest, decent people who mean well. It is the occasional negative or dishonest person who puts us on our guard with everyone.*

CHANGE OF TERRAIN

It was sundown when we got out of Tangiers once more, after having cooked our supper on the sidewalk while the radiator cooled, much to the amusement of the passers-by. There was no need to stop before Casablanca, we agreed; we had set ourselves a tentative schedule and were running half a day behind it.

It was 3 a.m. when we arrived outside Casablanca, blind, sleepy from the long day and night since Gibraltar. Fearful of cutthroats and thieves, with which the infamous city of intrigue and Casbah must surely be rife, we parked in the middle of a vast field, far from any buildings, and slept on and around our supplies rather than risk the ground outside.

Thus passed our first night in Africa. A small boy tending half a dozen sheep was the sole spectator to our advent from the Rover the next morning. Rubbing half a dozen spots where the corners of the boxes had dug into us in the night, we stretched and yawned in the warm sunshine, unloading a few cans of food for breakfast. Immediately after eating the beans and sausages, we drove into the busy city of modern skyscrapers and traffic jams, becoming lost minutes later in the search for a place to buy discount petrol coupons.

By the time we extricated ourselves from the maze of crowded, cobbled streets, we had the coupons and were on the road to Marrakesh. We were on our way at last.

The change in the people and the country from the day before in Gibraltar was profound. Gone were the trousers, shirts, and jackets of the European continent. In their places were the flowing robes and dark burnooses of Arabia, the women with their faces covered, except for a tiny patch over one eye, through which they peered at our passing. The old men in the rocky fields, tending sheep or hacking listlessly at stringy rows of corn, wore rolled headdresses, covering their ears and necks from the baking sun, merging into loose folds of cloth, enveloping the body and legs to the ankles, where gnarled feet protruded into rugged rope or leather sandals.

The sun was hotter than it had been the day before. The fields, except where some sort of primitive irrigation was in progress, were parched and yellow with thin, scrubby grass and the odd thorn tree. The occasional river was shallow and light brown with mud, undrinkable, flowing languorously between dusty banks lined with tired cypress trees. The countryside, from the ancient stone houses and crumbling fences to the worn footpaths winding away from the road into the rocky, lifeless country beyond, gave one the impression of uncaring timelessness.

The bicycle and the burro replaced the automobile as the common form of transportation. Clay and sticks replaced the bricks and mortar of Europe as the most popular building materials. Lassitude and passivity had settled over a land that had been poor for so long that the people accepted indigence and subsistence as a way of life, not to be questioned in this world. It was easy to understand how the Moslem law of Kismet ("Everything is written and cannot be changed—unless Allah wills it.") had been received and embraced so unquestioningly by these people.

Spain had been poor, with its peasants and third-class trains, its dirty streets and blackened cities, but what we were seeing was a poverty so deeply ingrained in the fiber and social structure of a land as to be unalterable. The people looked as though they had lived with it for so long that any other way of life would have been a step toward dissolution of their system, not progressive or even regressive, just a removal of the security they had in being poor, and expecting nothing more than a continuation of that insecurity. We had the feeling that, in our Land Rover, we were incomparably wealthy next to the citizens of the country, but that it didn't really matter much to them. It wasn't an affluence to gloat over or talk about; it was rather something to know, and to have, and not to make too much of.

Our beautiful, detailed, incredibly accurate map indicated three main routes across the Sahara, and we decided to remain with our original plan—to cross Morocco to the Sahara, cross the Sahara from Morocco through Spanish Morocco to Senegal, 1,800 miles beyond, and travel around the hump of Africa to Nigeria. This route went through almost every country in West Africa, over a distance of 5,000 miles, and was, as far as we could discern, the most interesting and comprehensive of the three routes available. Our goal for the day was Agadir, on the Atlantic coast in southern Morocco. Agadir would be our jumping-off place for the Sahara, which we considered to be not much more than a long, boring drive, to get behind us as quickly as possible.

In our urgent desire to make as many miles as possible each day, we drove steadily, stopping only for an hour at Marrakesh to eat our supper and refuel from the jerry cans. Then, we drove on through the night into the Atlas Mountains.

The road leading to the mountains is paved, as is the road leading to Tarroudant and Agadir from the other side. The 60 kilometers in between were the worst we had ever driven, taking two hours of jolting, bone-rattling fighting with the wheel and the gears to accomplish. Three times the radiator had to be topped up with water from the jerry cans, and we each took a turn driving, but the Rover responded beautifully the whole way. When we came back onto the decent road, shortly after midnight, it was with the beginning of a pride and affection for that vehicle that was to grow to an undying love. I look back on that Rover with love, as an older man might remember a childhood sweetheart.

But at that moment, we were again wilting from fatigue, and could think of little beyond getting to Agadir and getting some sleep. At 3 a.m. we drove through the musty streets of the city to the sea, and then along the sea road until we found a cliff high above the crashing surf. There, in a rocky field, we threw our bags on the ground and slept like babies.

The radiator had sprung a leak in the night, requiring a welding torch to seal, so that was the first business of the day. After breakfast in a goat-soiled alley, during which our two stoves blew up in flames, we sought out a workshop for the necessary repairs.

The French-Arab owner was very accommodating, and in addition to not charging us for the welding, he gave us some advice concerning our proposed route. The first, in which he was echoed by his partner, was that we should not attempt to cross the Sahara at that time of the year. It was too hot, they said. We would ruin our vehicle and have to leave it there. It was dangerous, as we knew nothing about desert traveling; and there was nothing to see there anyway.

We thanked him for his concern, expressing a friendly disinterest in his gloomy predictions. We weren't going to spend any more time than was absolutely necessary in the desert, we told him amiably. We were going to drive straight across to get to black Africa without further delay.

When he saw that we had no intention of heeding his warnings, he gave us another tidbit to think about. The Moroccans and the Algerians were embroiled in a border dispute in the area we'd be driving through that afternoon. Several soldiers had been killed in the past weeks arguing the point. If we must go, we had better visit the military headquarters in town and get a *laissez-passier* to allow us through the lines. That interested us a lot.

We didn't know very much about African politics, and we had no desire to become involved with them. This expedition, we agreed, was purely a friendly one, a gesture of goodwill, and any way to avoid involvement was the way for us. We drove straight from the workshop to army headquarters to get a pass to allow us through the disputed area.

We arrived just after midday on Saturday, but already the offices were closed, and would stay shut until Monday. Since we couldn't advance without the official authorization, we would have to wait until the offices reopened. That wasn't such an objectionable idea since hundreds of miles of sunny beaches stretched before us. We were, however, a bit perturbed at the delay, and the mess it made of our schedule, which called for 200 miles per day.

ALMOST HEAVEN

Ten miles up the coast from Agadir we found an uninhabited little cove embracing 100 yards of firm, clean sand, sheltered from the wind and invisible from the main road. It was the type of place the holiday brochures describe to lure the tourists to North Africa. The sun was warm and brightly beaming the whole day. And the privacy was above reproach; except for an occasional passing Arab on his drowsy burro, we didn't see another person all weekend. The water was lovely, like warm silk to swim in, and we forswore swimming trunks most of the time to cavort as close to nature as possible. In a place like that, at a time like that, it seemed that no price was too much to pay to be world-beaters. Except for one little detail, it was letter perfect. And that was the flies.

From the first tinge of sun in the eastern sky to the last streak of crimson on the western horizon, the flies were everywhere. In the morning, we would wake from the flies on our lips, around our eyes, and in our ears. We were beset by clouds of flies at every meal and throughout the day—buzzing, crawling, nibbling droves of irritating flies. Any activity that involved sitting in one place was undertaken with something in a free hand to wave back and forth in front of the face to keep the flies away. Conversation, viewed from a distance, looked like a waving game.

Hand waving the flies away, hands moving like a windshield wiper, soon became a part of life in North Africa, as regular as breathing. We became accustomed to the flies after a while, like one does to a plaster cast on a broken limb. We were always happy when the setting sun drew them away, not to be seen again until the crack of dawn the following morning.

Whenever you embark on any new endeavor, you will be beset by countless little problems, details, unexpected irritations, difficult and dishonest people of all kinds. They go with the territory. They are an unavoidable part of the price you have to pay to accomplish anything new or worthwhile. This is probably what William James of Harvard meant when he wrote, "The first step in dealing with any difficulty is to be willing to have it so."

We were up with the sun, and the flies, on Monday morning, eager to continue on our way into Africa. We took an invigorating swim to wake up, knowing that it would be almost a week, according to our calculations, before we would reach the sea below the Sahara, in Senegal, on the other side of the desert.

The Map, Radiator, and Warnings

Call it luck or fate or a manifestation of brotherly love—but *so often the one thing you need most at the moment is provided, providentially, to prepare you for the next stage.* Without the map and the economical repair of the radiator, we certainly would have perished in the Sahara Desert. And every experience, no matter how unexpected or frustrating, was teaching us something we would need to know in the fullness of time.

CHAPTER 13

THE BEST-LAID PLANS OF MICE AND MEN

At 8 a.m. we drove up the gravel driveway to the military administration building, taking our map and a French dictionary to explain what we wanted. It took a little sign language and word hunting to send the message to the unshaved Moroccan soldier on the front steps that we would like to see an official of some sort to procure a *laisser-passer* for the frontier. We were eventually ushered into a bare office with only a desk and two chairs for furniture. One of the chairs was generously filled with a large, fretful captain.

The answer we received was equally bare. The border was closed. There was no possibility of our passing through the disputed zone. It was too dangerous. If the Moroccans didn't shoot us going, the Algerians would probably shoot us coming. He was polite, concise, and busy. We would have to find another route.

"Well, that was quick," said Bob. "What do we do now?"

"Like the man says, we have to find another route."

Alas! It was one of the ups and downs of world-beating. But why did we seem to be getting all the downs? Huddled in the Land Rover over the map, six weeks of tentative planning dashed in six minutes of Moroccan officialdom, we glumly worked out another plan.

The second trans-Saharan route on our map was through Algeria, across the heart of the desert, and into Mali, continuing along the Niger River into Dahomey and eventually into Nigeria. To intersect this route in the shortest distance, we would follow a series of ragged roads 400 miles eastwards, across the Moroccan hinterland to the border with Algeria, at a town called Figuig—then we would turn south toward Nigeria again.

Coming to Agadir had been a waste of four days, 600 miles worth of petrol, and one eighth of our supplies. To go back involved a long, hard drive.

"It's sure as hell a long way to Tipperary," said Geoff, folding the map so our route was exposed.

"With average speed, we can be in Algeria in 20 hours," I calculated. "The sooner we get started, the sooner we get finished."

"Oh crap!" said Bob. "That means we're going to have to drive all night again. What point is there in that?"

"We're behind schedule, Bob," said Geoff. "We've got to make up the time we've lost, and then we've got to make up the time we're losing while we're making up the time we've lost."

"Yeah, what could be simpler than that?"

Geoff eased out the clutch and steered the Rover back onto the main road. The sun was already beginning to beat down through the canvas top, making the inside of the vehicle stifling hot when it wasn't moving. It was, indeed, a long way to Tipperary.

One hour out of Agadir, we pulled off the road into an olive grove and ran the Rover into the shade to cool. The ignition was acting up, a combination of contacts and overheating, we thought, and decided to cure both at the same time. When the engine cooled, we put in a set of heavy-duty points we had bought in Gibraltar, a special type we had never seen before, and never looked at them again after installing them. The sun was amazingly intense, broiling the air even in the shade, convincing us that driving was not a good idea until later in the afternoon.

A SOBERING DETOUR

Soon after starting again, we were passed by a large Land Rover, having as passengers the two girls to whom we had given a ride from the ferry in Tangiers four days previously.

Recognition was simultaneous, and we both stopped to exchange greetings. They were driving from the railhead in Agadir with a sturdy-looking English woman, and were on their way to Tarroudant, about 30 kilometers farther. There, they would work with blind children for the summer. They asked if we would like to follow along and come in for a cup of tea.

Forty minutes later, we entered the mud-walled city and followed the other vehicle closely through the narrow, sinister streets. Deep in the town, it stopped at a large gate in the wall surrounding an old Moorish house. The gate was opened by an ancient Arab, who closed it behind us when we had entered into the flag-stoned courtyard.

The house was built of mud bricks in a box shape around a small lawn, fringed with flowers. It had high ceilings done in mosaic and was wonderfully cool inside. On either side of the courtyard were blooming orange trees in neat rows, on a carpet of lush grass. I couldn't help but think that it was a lovely place for a blind children's orphanage.

"Blindness," said Miss Waltars, as she poured the mint tea into tiny cups, "is considered a curse, put on a family by Allah. If it has not cleared up by the time the child is five, they believe the only way to lift the curse is to do away with the child."

"You don't mean a family will actually kill its children, do you?"

"Yes," she replied. "It's quite common in Arab lands. However, often the child is taken into the country and abandoned to die of starvation and exposure."

"Surely there must be some law against that sort of thing," said Geoff. "Isn't there any way of stopping it?"

"Oh yes," she said, "the police watch out for it. Most of our children have been brought here at the insistence of the police, or after the children have been found wandering or been terribly beaten and left for dead."

"Why don't the parents bring the children here?" Bob asked.

"We've been trying to encourage that for six years now," Miss Waltars explained. "But they feel that we are somehow contradicting their beliefs, and they rarely do."

At that moment, the door opened from the courtyard, and a line of young Arab children were shepherded patiently into the room by the old fellow who had opened the gate for us. Their clothes were old, but neat and clean, and their little faces all brightened when Miss Waltars called out to them in Arabic. There were boys and girls, ranging in age from five to eleven, and by their glassy, inconsistent stares, it was immediately apparent that they were all blind.

"This is Freddy," said Miss Waltars, gathering one of the little boys into her arms. "He had a particularly bad time of it before we got to him, didn't you, Freddy?"

The little boy obviously didn't understand the words, but his face beamed a joyous grin toward the sound of the voice.

"His grandmother brought him to us after he'd been beaten terribly and left to the wild dogs outside the city gates. We didn't think he was going to live, but he fooled us."

Freddy came to the sound of our voices and shook hands with each of us in turn. His face was lined with scars from recently healed cuts, and one arm was encased in plaster. But even with the scars and the blank gaze, his face was beaming with happiness.

After the children were led into the garden to play on the grass before dinner, we rose and excused ourselves, thanking Miss Waltars for the tea and a very enlightening visit. We wished the girls a good summer at the same time and assured them we could find our way out of the city.

When we left that orphanage, we drove in silence until we were back on the road and heading away from Tarroudant.

"It would be interesting to know just how much goes on under the surface that you never even hear about," said Geoff, breaking the silence.

"Look at those girls back there," said Bob, "ready to spend the whole summer taking care of those kids, just for the sake of doing it. Makes a guy feel kind of useless."

"Yeah, and that's the kind of thing you never hear about young people doing. All you get in the papers are stories about protest marchers and gang wars."

"Yes, it's true," said Geoff. "Gives one something to think about, doesn't it?"

I learned, as I thought more about it, that *much good happens in this world is never recognized, reported, or rewarded. And many of the true heroes and heroines are humble men and women who serve others unselfishly, one day at a time.*

A HARD DAY'S NIGHT

We turned off the main road onto gravel just as the sun set. Two hours later we were hopelessly lost in a maze of cart tracks, creek beds, and what appeared to be roads through the rocky brushland, but were really just dead ends. The four-wheel drive of the Rover dragged us across washouts as wide as 300 yards and up the far sides to continue on the footpaths and goat trails. Shortly before 11 p.m., after going around in circles for hours, we straggled onto a well-graveled road and came upon a sign that informed us of how far we hadn't come that evening. Half an hour later, the right front tire went flat, and we lurched to a dull halt. It was turning out to be a good night all around.

This presented us with a little problem. Because the cheapest tires in Gibraltar had been selling at eight pounds each, we had chosen to ignore the fact that only two of our tires were half decent. The four pound price tag on the cheapest jack we had looked at disinclined us from adding that instrument to our tool box before we left. We hadn't bought a wrench for the lug nuts either. Except that we had a spare tire, we couldn't have been less prepared for flats if we had made an effort.

But we weren't lacking in imagination. With a heave-ho and a grunt, we lifted the front of the Rover onto three jerry cans, suspending the guilty wheel. While Bob unbolted the spare tire from the hood and Geoff prepared tea, I experimented with various methods of removing rusty lug nuts without the proper wrench. There aren't any. Especially in the middle of nowhere, in the middle of the night.

We had to rely on the next motorist, and the code of the road, the creed by which we traveled. It was a simple, unspoken, reciprocal agreement ruling the conduct of drivers in less populated areas. *If we saw someone with difficulties, we stopped and did our best to help them, and in turn, we reaped the benefits of someone stopping for us when we had problems,* as we did at that moment. In the driving we had done in northern British Columbia, and all across North America, in the rural areas especially, we had come to accept this code as a responsibility of driving, as much so as the dimming of our headlights in the face of oncoming traffic. In that lonely spot, we had no doubt that this code would be honored; it was merely a question of when the next vehicle would come along and whether it would contain the necessary tool. By driving thousands of miles, we had joined a brotherhood of the road, and since we had always paid our dues, we had no fear of being ignored by one of the fraternal members.

The water for tea was beginning to steam when the first oncoming vehicle appeared in the distant blackness. It was 15 minutes later before the vehicle, a bus, came over the rise and bore down upon us where we stood drinking tea.

The bus came to a smooth halt 20 feet from the rear of our Rover, holding us and our teacups in its bright headlamps. I went to the door and explained our difficulty to the burly driver, and asked him if he might have the correct wrench. He nodded, assuring me that he had a large tool box, and then cut the engine. Turning to the passengers, he said something in Arabic and chuckled, at which the passengers chuckled in agreement and started leaving their seats to get off the bus, for natural reasons.

As the driver and his assistant busied themselves with the tool box, locked under the luggage compartment on the outside of the bus, the passengers, all men in various types of dress, filed off the bus and casually dispersed themselves. The driver found a T-bar tire wrench and went to the front of the Rover to try it. We followed behind to do the work if it was the correct tool. It was the right tool, but the driver of the bus and his helper refused to accept our offer, jokingly insisting that they take care of it. There was nothing to do under the circumstances but to pour another cup of tea.

In the glow of the lights from the tail lamps of the Rover and the parking globes of the bus, the passengers had gathered and now sat, or stood, conversing quietly or looking on with curious expressions. Several had squatted on their heels, and three or four sat cross-legged, Indian fashion, in their suits or robes.

Two old men, however, lay out on the ground with their hands on their chins, watching us interestedly and talking to each other in little whispers. These two looked exactly like grizzled old hounds curled before a fire, lying there on the road. The soft sounds of the tire-changing in the background created a rather eerie, though peaceful, atmosphere. Around the vehicles surged the silence and darkness of the balmy summer night, like a breathless sea hugging around a small island, held in position by chains of warm velvet. Overhead, the sky was a sheet of tiny stars, sparkling faintly in the blackened heavens. It felt like a spell cast over us in the stillness, hinting at eternity. We leaned on the Rover and sipped the tea without speaking.

The spell was broken by the laughing of the driver at the jerry cans that were substituting for a jack. We put down our cups and took up positions along the bumper, lifting the Rover and dropping it squarely on the road. The driver and the passengers gave a delighted cheer and happily climbed back onboard the bus. We offered the driver a cup of tea, but he laughed and just shook hands, declining the tea and taking his place behind the wheel. With a roar and a beep-beep, the bus crept away, picked up speed, and lumbered smoothly down the road into the night.

From start to finish, the episode had taken less than 10 minutes. Once again we were alone with the night, by the darkened tailgate, each with a cup of tea in hand, and a long, long way from home.

THE LAW OF RECIPROCITY

You will find with experience that this is one of the greatest of all principles for success and happiness. This law flows from the Law of Sowing and Reaping, which says, "Whatsoever a man soweth, that also shall he reap."

In day-to-day life, whatever you sow, you reap. Whatever you are reaping today is a result of what you have sown in the past. And there's no escaping!

Whatever you do for others will eventually be done for you, "pressed down, shaken and overflowing."

The more of yourself and your resources you give away with no expectation of return, the more will come back to you from the most unexpected sources, and in the most remarkable ways.

Always be looking for ways to give, to contribute to others. The rewards will flow back to you with the force and power of Universal Law.

CHAPTER 14

A CHANGE OF PACE

The dawn found us driving steadily eastward through desolate land. We had crossed the Atlas Mountains again in the night and now they rose bare and forbidding, far to the north. To the east, the south and the west, the rolling terrain extended to the far horizon, unbroken by trees, or hills, or salient objects of any kind. The entire landscape was covered with a gray-black rocky gravel, settled close upon the earth, allowing only an occasional tuft of hardy grass through its roughened surface. The road was merely a well-marked track, scraped clear of loose stones to lessen the destructive force on the passing vehicles.

There was an aura of primitive beauty about it. Even though we were chilled by the cold of early morning, hungry and tired from the long night, we couldn't help but feel a trifle awed by the stark simplicity of that empty land.

"This is the northernmost reach of the Sahara," said Geoff, opening the map to its full length. "But we still have to go another 500 miles south before the real desert begins."

"If it's like this here," said Bob, "what will it be like in the middle of the desert?"

"It'll probably be the dullest land on earth," I said. "We'll get across it as quickly as we can, that's for sure."

"Yes," agreed Geoff. "We didn't come to this continent to see the Sahara—it's just something in the way. The sooner we get it behind us, the better."

"I wonder," muttered Bob, "just what we did come to this continent to see."

"Black Africa, old buddy. That's what. And it won't be long now."

Except for the odd goat herders and their tiny flocks, feeding off God only knows what, the few inhabitants of that region lived in small towns older than history. These mud-bricked clusters of dwellings, often surrounded with high walls, were invariably built around an oasis, visible from many miles off by the bright green of the tall date palms. The life-giving water came from wells dug deep in the clay beside parched creek beds, and was hauled by hand or treadmill, to be spilled carefully into the closely watched vegetable gardens. The hardness of the life was etched into the faces of the old men and women who raised their heads mutely at the sound of our vehicle, and just as silently returned to their endless toil. We were only a two-day drive from Europe, but it seemed we were in a land that time had forgotten.

The first large oasis we reached that morning had one lonely petrol station where we had our tire repaired before continuing. The first town we passed through of any size was Ksar-es-Souk, shortly before midday. Ten kilometers later we were blessed with our second flat tire, and sat down resignedly to wait for the next motorist.

An Arab-driven, weather-beaten old dump truck came along the dirt road half an hour later, the smiling driver stopping and getting out automatically to see why we were waiting. He gladly loaned us the large wrench and drove off casually when we had completed the job. Better safe than sorry, we figured, and returned to Ksar-es-Souk to have the flat repaired before continuing.

Compared to the relative bustle of the dusty little town an hour before, it was empty and silent when we drove to the tire shop we had seen on the main square. All the shops were closed and shuttered, as was the tire shop, so we parked the Rover and sat in the shade of a small café to wait. It was obviously lunch time, and the town would be open in another few minutes.

The cold Coca-Cola mentioned in the cracked window of the café turned out to be warm, but the proprietor was a friendly fellow so we didn't complain. My knowledge of French had progressed to the stage of being able to ask simple questions and understand simpler answers, so I asked the fellow just when the shops would reopen.

"Oh," he said, "not long."

"About what time, exactly?"

"Oh, perhaps 4 p.m., perhaps 5 p.m."

It was then just after 1 p.m.

"All stores are closed in the afternoons," he said.

Well, that was just dandy. We would have to revel in the joys of sitting and waiting for the next few hours.

We had been driving more or less steadily, or been away from the towns, in our first five days in Morocco, and this was our first exposure to the profound change in the way of life necessitated by the extreme heat of the desert regions. We were to find that throughout North Africa and the Sahara, during the hours when the sun is at its zenith, all work and most activity comes to a standstill. To compensate for this, the working day begins early, at

6 or 7 a.m., and continues from reopening time, usually 4 p.m., until 7 or 8 p.m.

The four or five hours in the middle of the day are spent in noisy cafés blaring Arab music, in bed sleeping, or in some other pursuit requiring a minimum of effort. Rarely will one see a vehicle on the road during the searing heat of midday because of the danger of blown head gaskets, or the oil in the crankcase thinning to the point where it no longer provides sufficient lubrication. At that point, the engine seizes up, and the car never runs again. Many people had perished that way. It began to dawn on us that there was a lot more to this Sahara crossing than rough roads and passport stamps.

It took us a long time to get over the hurry-up, right-now attitude we had brought with us; in fact, we never did completely shake off the sense of urgency that accompanied everything we attempted. We did adapt, however, to an amazing degree, to the unhurried way of life around us.

But at that moment, we were fresh from 20 years of "not now, but right now!" and we couldn't help but fret when we were delayed. No one seemed to understand that we were in a hurry; we had a schedule to make, places to go, things to do. To us, procrastination was an evil. But, to the world we now found ourselves in, it was as natural as the midday heat. Waiting three hours in Ksar-es-Souk to have a tire repaired was the beginning of a gradual realization of what we had bitten off in coming to Africa, and in the long run, it made everything just a little bit easier to chew.

PACE YOURSELF

Successful people tend to be action-oriented. They have a sense of urgency. They want to get on with the job, to get it done, to get on to the next thing.

But the majority move at a much slower pace. They see little need for speed. They take their time and work at their own pace.

One of the basic principles is that "People don't change." *Part of being flexible and adaptive is for you to pace yourself as well. Slow down when you have to. Don't allow yourself to become tense or anxious.*

As the Bible says, "There is a time for every purpose under heaven." Sometimes the smartest thing you can do is to just "go with the flow."

CHAPTER 15

YOU WILL DIE IN THE DESERT

At this point we began to have an experience that was repeated in different ways throughout the trip. One of the Arabs asked us where we were going. We told him we were going across the Sahara and south into Africa.

He said, "Oh no, you can't do that. You'll die in the desert." He said it with such conviction and finality that I wasn't sure I had understood the French words.

I asked him to repeat, "Vous allez mourir dans le désert." We assumed he was just joking, or perhaps this was a common way of greeting desert travelers.

Later, however, he brought over a couple of Arab friends and introduced us as the young men who were going off to "die in the desert." They seemed quite cheerful, as if we had said we were going to Disneyland, but we were a trifle irritated.

From then on, whenever we would say we were crossing the Sahara, they would immediately respond, "Non, non; vous allez mourir dan les désert."

And by the way, these were not just city Arabs or town dwellers. Often they were Taureq or Bedouin, people whose ancestors had lived in the Sahara for 1,000 years. They were in a position to know.

I learned later that *whenever you think about trying something new or different or unusual, people will line up to tell you that you can't do it, you'll fail, you'll lose your money or time or investment, that "you'll die in the desert."*

To succeed at anything, *you have to learn to ignore the naysayers, the negative people, many of whom should know better. You must have the courage to step out in faith, with no guarantees of success, to rise above all resistance and press on regardless.*

The country we were going through had gradually changed from stony terrain to scrub brush and rocky waste in the driving between sunrise and noon. After we left Ksar-es-Souk, the repaired tire firmly bolted to the hood, the country changed again, becoming more rugged and overgrown with heavier sagebrush. In the late afternoon, we crossed two shallow rivers, the roadway marked by boulders spaced a few feet apart in the water. The deepest part was just over two feet, but the Land Rover waded through it like a sturdy little freight boat as water gurgled through the doors onto the floor. There didn't seem to be anywhere that vehicle couldn't go.

BOB BECOMES ILL

After Boudenib, 60 kilometers from Ksar-es-Souk, the country flattened out again, and the bad road became worse. To add to the pounding we were enduring from the ungraded track and the wind that was making the cooking of our unimaginative supper almost impossible, Bob had become violently ill. His stomach had started to bother him the evening before, after supper, and he had been unable to do more than pick at breakfast. Geoff and I didn't think too much about it, except to observe that if Bob didn't eat his share, there was more food for us.

The long day from Agadir, and then the rough night on the broken roads, followed by the long hot day that was just ending, had destroyed Bob's body's resistance to illness. His whole system seemed to be out of kilter—head, stomach, and bowels. He was bringing up everything he ate or drank, even water, and he was afflicted with dysentery so persistent and painful that we were stopping every few minutes to let him out of the Rover, fumbling frantically at his pants as he dashed to the side of the road. He was dizzy and his head was pounding crazily, his face white and filmed with cold perspiration. Whatever he had, he had it in a bad way, and there was nothing we could do about it, except drive on.

Aside from a few bandages and a box of aspirin, we had no medical supplies whatsoever, having felt that we were too healthy to worry about disease, dysentery, diarrhea, or even severe pain. Geoff and I had taken first aid courses and passed at the top of the class, but we were not prepared for something like this. The only answer was to get to Figuig as fast as possible, and hope to find a doctor or someone who could prescribe a medicine for him.

But Figuig was still many hours away, and we couldn't continue in our exhausted condition without eating something. We tried to keep our kerosene burner lit by placing it in a gully, but the wind gusted nastily from all angles, carrying sand and grit into the food and blowing out the flame so often that we finally gave up and ate the slop cold. Morbidly tired, caked with sweat and dirt from the road, the cold supper still gritty in our mouths, Geoff and I made a place for Bob to lay in the back of the Rover, and we continued on.

That was a bad night. It started off with Bob sick and all of us dead tired, and it got worse, as the road deteriorated to nothing within a couple of hours. It seemed as though the blackened country was crisscrossed with tracks that confused us and left us hopelessly lost, time after time. Having no idea of where we were on the map, we resorted to using our compass, as well as a couple of stars, to keep going in the general direction of east, hoping to cross the north-south track to Figuig and get our bearings once more. But the impassability of the rocky terrain kept turning us around, sending us off on diverse tangents, while the broken ground underneath threatened to shake the laboring vehicle and us into pieces. Fighting the road, the wheel and the gears was a Herculean effort, forcing us to change drivers every half hour.

Our speed was never more than 25 or 30 miles per hour, but hitting a washout or a small crevice, even at that low speed, would cause the vehicle to bounce off the ground and come hammering back down, bringing moans and curses from the suffering Bob in the back, and bringing our taut nerves to the snapping point. At every hard bump, we'd slow and proceed more carefully, hunched forward tensely for the next surprise.

From Bad to Worse

The headlights played tricks on us repeatedly, hiding large ruts in shadows and making smooth stretches appear dangerous. We'd been driving for six jarring hours and struggling to focus our bleary eyes on the ground ahead. When we came over a rise, suddenly the road was gone!

I slammed on the brakes desperately, but it was too late. We plunged off a riverbank and slammed into the opposite bank, coming to a sudden halt. Bob was hurled out of the back of the Rover right onto our heads. For a second we just sat there, all tangled up in each other, almost without the energy to move. We were sure that the whole front end of our vehicle was ruined.

Wearily, Geoff and I untangled ourselves from the moaning Bob, and crawled out to take a look at the situation. Bob leaned his head out the door from where he lay and retched hollowly, gagging from the emptiness of his stomach. The headlights were still on, murky against the dust rising from the collision with the bank. The only sound was the wind whistling through the dry sagebrush that bordered the gully in which we had landed.

Thank God for small favors and single-unit construction, we muttered tiredly. The heavy steel bumper was solidly into the clay bank, but there wasn't a scratch on the vehicle. Bob shakily climbed into the back of the Rover again while I tried the motor. It started with a hollow pop and ran smoothly. Shoving it into four-wheel drive, I backed it out of the dirt and then followed Geoff's flashlight to get out of the gully. Geoff got wearily into the Rover and slouched back, watching the illuminated road ahead.

"You know something," he sighed. "We've let ourselves in for far more than we realized with this Africa idea."

"What do you mean, Geoff?" I let out the clutch and we started slowly forward. "Well, just look at us in comparison to a year ago," he said. "Here we are in the middle of nowhere, lost, beat as hell, with Bob sick as a dog, and 8,000 miles to go. And we've only really been in Africa for a week. Where's it going to lead to?"

"It'll be interesting to find out. I don't even want to take a guess, except South Africa."

"Yeah," he said. "That's something, anyway."

We drove cautiously for the next hour and finally intersected the long-sought road to Figuig. According to the map there was only one road. We turned left in the direction of the north star. At the most, Figuig could only be a couple of hours farther, but we were dead tired. Bob had finally fallen asleep, and there was no reason to go on anymore. I coasted the vehicle off the road into the brush and cut the engine.

"We're home," I said, but Geoff was already dragging his sleeping bag out of the back. Within a minute, we were sprawled in our bags on the sandy ground and fast asleep.

LAST DAY IN MOROCCO

It was 9 a.m. when we stirred from our beds on the dirt, awakened by the passing of a truck full of Arab workers, all shouting at us. Bob had improved considerably with sleep, but he still couldn't look at breakfast. He was a bit shaky on his feet and very pale, like a man who had been terribly frightened and hadn't quite regained his composure.

Owing to our loss of direction in the night, we had come on to the gravel road much farther from Figuig than we had calculated, twice as far in fact. It was shortly after 1 p.m. when we arrived in the little, unpaved border town and drove up to the old building with the Moroccan flag in front. We were informed that we had to be checked out of Morocco before entering Algeria, and the man in charge would not be back until 3 p.m. We got out the makings for tea and Geoff set to it.

At first we tried to keep the stove going on the tailgate of the Rover, but there was too much wind. Instead, we set the cheap contraption on the ground-level porch of the customs building, lit it, and set the kettle on to boil. Several curious Arabs, who had been lounging around the building, gathered to stare at us and observe the tea-making operation, as simple as it was. The decrepit stove picked this particular occasion to put on a show.

We had leaned the wooden top from a packing crate against the stove from one side to stop the wind, and the seam on that side burst from the pressure of gasoline dribbling down the side and ignited. In seconds, the ground around and under the wooden crate was aflame, black smoke billowing up around the kettle. As more gasoline joined the fire, the smoke increased in density, enveloping the stove and sending the flames up two feet.

The Arabs became quite concerned, pointing to the stove and jabbering excitedly, offering advice on how to extinguish the little inferno that had now obscured the stove and kettle and was filling the verandah with oily smoke.

Then suddenly the bottom of the stove and the remaining petrol went up with an ominous woosh, causing the onlooking Arabs to jump back in fright. The smoke filled the little porch even thicker than before, swirling in the gusty breeze and pouring over the brick wall next to it.

Geoff had completed the laying out of the cups, the teapot, the sugar, and a can of evaporated milk on the tailgate, and with a nonchalant smile at the Arabs, he strolled casually into the blazing cloud and plucked the blackened kettle from the flames. Just as casually, he strolled back and made the tea, with a bored look at the astonished locals. I yawned and turned a nearby hose on the fire, dousing it and cooling the misshapen lump of metal that had been the stove. Then, picking it up as though it were a valuable instrument, I wiped it off a bit with a piece of paper and set it back in the Rover. Bob was sitting in the front seat, glumly reading about scaramouche, and didn't even bother looking up.

We managed to convey to the Arabs that this was our normal way of making tea—you had to smoke it. From their huddled chatter and bewildered expressions, we got the impression that it was not done that way in Figuig.

ANOTHER WRONG TURN

The captain in charge of customs arrived at 3:30 and examined all our papers before stamping us out of the country. After the handshaking routine with the entire office staff, about six of them telling us we would die in the desert, we were directed toward the east end of town and told that Algeria was thataway. There were two roads leading in the general direction of east, and with that unerring sense of path-finding, inherent in us pioneers from the west, we took the wrong one.

The street soon became too tight for us to turn around, narrowing to a passage just wide enough for the Rover, and then turned sharply down a steep slope.

In an attempt to turn the Rover around in the narrow street, we became stuck. The engine stalled and wouldn't restart. We got out and tried pushing the vehicle back and forward, but to no avail. We were stuck fast.

Almost immediately, the street filled with curious young men and boys, dressed much alike in baggy pantaloons and worn, buttonless shirts. (Aha! The necessary labor force is at hand.)

(What are they staring at? Why don't they offer to push? How do you say "push" in Arabic? Maybe they need a little encouragement. Yeah, let's set them a good example.)

With dumb smiles, we weakly gave the Rover a couple of useless shoves, laughing foolishly and motioning to everyone that they could play, too. They thought it was a splendid idea, and the entire crowd—about 20 men in all—clustered around the vehicle and started pushing in all directions. We laughed and waved them to the front end, chanting in French, "un, deux, trois—and shove, un, deux, trois—and shove."

Everyone picked it up, and the street filled with cheering and grunting, the Rover dislodging on the third heave. During the round of applause and congratulations the man gave each other, we fiddled with the electric fuel pump and got the engine started again, with a sigh of relief.

We had to back all the way up the street we'd come down, beeping the horn and waving to the gang chasing along in front. They wanted to play "Push the Happy Green Land Rover" again. This time we took the right road, which ended at the edge of town and came, a few minutes later, to the guarded frontier of Algeria. Our Morocco days were at an end.

PATIENCE IS A VIRTUE

There is a time for urgency and aggressive action, and there is a time for patience.

Many of your decisions will turn out to be wrong. The smartest thing you can do in many cases is to stop and reconsider. Slow down. Think it through. Develop alternatives.

Then, take a deep breath, smile, relax, and be patient with the fact that not everything happens at the time and speed you desire.

Henry Ford once said, "Patience and foresight are vital for success, and the man who lacks patience is not cut out for responsibilities in business."

Be cool. Go slow. Take it easy. Everything is probably unfolding as it should, in its right time.

CHAPTER 16

ALGERIA AND THE SAHARA

In both directions, as far as we could see, the barbed wire of the disputed border blocked off any thought of entering Algeria at this point. It was about 50 yards from one side to the other and very impressive to us, we not having seen anything of its sort before.

The first 10 yards were a mass of barbed, coiled loops about 10 feet high, with three barbed-wire fences running parallel through them about six feet apart. Then came a cleared space, 30 yards in width, with a single 12-foot high, electrified fence running down the center on heavy cement posts. The other side of this no man's land was bordered with another mass of the terrible-looking strands. At intervals of 200 yards, on the other side of the wire frontier, the ugly faces of concrete pillboxes glared at the palm trees of Morocco.

Although there was no road leading up to it, our map indicated that there was a way somewhere, and since one direction was as good as another, we turned right and followed the wire south. It had been a good guess, for three kilometers along we came to a channel leading in to the wire and up to an electrified gate.

Two dirty soldiers pointed machine pistols at us, while a third swung the gate open and motioned for us to enter. Once we were inside the canyon of barbed wire, the two soldiers flanked our vehicle, weapons drawn, while we drove at a walking speed along the narrow alley to the next gate. We had no inclination to drive any faster than they wanted us to.

On the far side of the second gate, two more Algerians waited with machine pistols to assure that we didn't overrun their country. We were ordered out of the Rover while they briefly inspected it for contraband Moroccans, and then ordered us to follow another car to headquarters, about three blocks into town. With all that hardware around, they didn't need to order. The slightest suggestion would have been quite sufficient.

With the aid of our map, we answered all their questions concerning our route and destination, obviously to their satisfaction, for we were soon allowed to proceed. We were told, however, that we would have to obtain Algerian visas in Colomb-Béchar, the next town south, immediately upon our arrival. We assured them that we would be there within two hours, and most certainly would comply with the request. After pumping up one of our tires at the air hose outside, we drove south from Beni-Ounif on the first paved road we'd seen since Tarroudant, three days before.

The paved road also confirmed a suspicion we had formed regarding our front end being damaged from the bank we'd hit in Morocco the night before. The steering wheel had been more difficult to handle. Halfway to Béchar, we stopped to check a grinding sound coming from the front tires, and we were chagrined to find that the rubber was scraping off at an alarming rate. In fact, there was no tread left, and it was obvious at once that the wheels were toeing in, due to something being broken or bent in the front suspension. We drove slowly the remainder of the way.

A well-dressed Algerian flagged us down as we approached Colomb-Béchar, explaining that he was from the police and had been informed from Beni-Ounif of our arrival. He led us into town to the police station, and taking our passports, told us to return the next morning with 14 dinars each (about $3) for our visas.

We were to learn later that visas were a serious business indeed. Throughout Europe, visas are not required to pass from one country to another, but once you get into Africa, the correct visa, stamped into your passport, makes the difference between entry and rejection. The absence of a visa can lead to arrest or detention, as we were to learn later.

In life, there are critical skills and information that are like visas. They make the difference between success and failure. And ignorance of them does not excuse you from the consequences of their absence.

Since our two front tires were now completely bald, we could not avoid the sad fact that we needed four tires and a spare if we were going to continue, and that meant procuring two more tires immediately, if not sooner. It was late afternoon, and all the shops in the small town were open. But neither of the two tire shops in Béchar had used tires for Land Rovers, and the price they were asking for new tires was a whopping $42 each. Each shop had one tire that fit our vehicle, and we decided to have one tire installed before driving out of town to make camp for the night. We had a lot of discussing to do.

Sitting by the Rover in a small grove of palm trees, we worked out our position on paper as of that moment. The situation was definitely not good. We were almost out of money. The ferry had cost $50, the insurance another $48, the food $100, and after buying gasoline and oil for 1,200 miles in Morocco, another stove, tire repairs, and the radiator, we were down to $150 when we reached Béchar. The $42 for the tire had dropped the total to $108 at that moment, and the bad news was just beginning.

BOB BAILS OUT, FOR GOOD

The following morning, we would have to pay $9 for visas and another $42 for the second tire. If we forswore the needed repairs and took a chance on the tires lasting, we would have just over $60. We needed a wrench for the wheel nuts and enough gasoline for 2,200 miles, the distance to Lagos. The gasoline alone in Morocco and Algeria cost more than $1 a gallon. Even if we averaged 25 miles to the gallon, we would need a minimum of $100 to reach Lagos. There was simply no way it could be done.

"Well," said Bob. "That is the end of that."

"What are you talking about?"

"We've had it; that's all," he replied. "The whole thing's been an abortion from start to finish—and the end is now."

"Just because we're a little low on money? We're not broke yet, you know."

"No, we're not broke," he sniffed. "We've got enough to get back to Gibraltar and sell the Land Rover, and we've got no other choice. I say we leave first thing in the morning."

"Bob, old buddy, this is a discussion to find a way to go on, not back. We've come too far to go back."

"The hell we have!" he replied. "It's on paper in front of you. We can't go on."

"What's your opinion on this, Geoff?"

"Now there's a question," he said, picking up the poetry book beside him. "Would you like to hear a poem?"

"What kind of a poem?" I already knew.

Ignoring the question, he began to read from "Carry On" by Robert W. Service.

> It's easy to fight when everything's right,
> When you're mad with the thrill and glory.
> It's easy to cheer when victory is near
> And wallow in fields that are gory.
> It's a different song when everything's wrong,
> When you're feeling infernally mortal.
> When it's ten against one and hope there is none,
> Buck up little soldier and chortle,

Carry on, carry on! There isn't much punch in your blow
You're glaring and staring and hitting out blind,
You're muddy and bloody but never you mind,
Carry on, carry on. You haven't the ghost of a show.
It's looking like death, but while you've a breath,
Carry on, my son, carry on.

Geoff closed the book with deliberation and spoke to Bob.

"That's how I feel, Bob. For the first time in my life, I've really got a little despair and defeat to contend with. We didn't expect this trip to be easy. If we'd thought it would be easy, we would not have come. And if we quit now, not only do we let ourselves down, but we also let Jack Turing down, and that I won't do. There has to be a way to get to Johannesburg, and no matter what challenge we face, that's where I'm going."

Geoff and I agreed that Johannesburg was our goal, regardless of the difficulties that cropped up on the way. "Surely, if we're determined enough, we'll find a way," I said.

"Do you know something?" Bob spoke slowly and distinctly. "You're both crazy. You read a stupid poem, and you're too blind to admit you're beaten. I'm not interested in this idiotic idea anymore. When you stop fooling yourselves, you'll see that I'm right. But I've had enough; I'm leaving for Gibraltar tomorrow morning."

Try as we may, this time we couldn't change his mind.

After cashing the rest of the travelers checks at the bank the next morning, we left the Rover to have the second tire fitted and walked over to the police station to retrieve our passports. On the way back to the vehicle, we stopped and bought a wrench to fit the wheel nuts. We were probably going to need it.

While we waited for the tire, Bob resolutely packed his rucksack with his belongings and one week's worth of tinned food. Geoff gave him $9 in Moroccan and Algerian money, the most we were willing to spare, leaving us with exactly $50.

Bob refused to change his mind. The bout with dysentery had taken the spirit out of him, and he wanted nothing more than to get back to England and forget this trip had ever happened. Geoff and I were, on one hand, sorry to see the end of such a long friendship, but on the other hand, we were glad to be rid of the voice of dissent and pessimism. It was a mixed emotion that actually left us neutral. We were thinking more of the road ahead, and what we would have to do to keep from going back to Gibraltar.

Since Bob had decided to hitchhike back to Gibraltar, we drove him to the main highway on the outskirts of town and let him off with his heavy pack.

"You sure you won't change your mind, Bob?"

"You should change yours," he said.

"Bob, old friend, do you really think that we won't make it? Do you think we could ever quit without making it?"

He looked at us carefully for a few seconds. "Ah, you'll make it, all right. I know you'll make it, somehow. But I'm just not interested anymore."

"So long, Bob. Say hello to Gibraltar for us."

We made a U-turn on the empty highway and drove back into town.

After receiving the money from Jack Turing and before leaving Gibraltar, we had rewritten to three or four people, affirming our requests for loans and asking that they send them to us in care of Barclays Bank, Lagos. We also left the address of Poste Restaunte, Lagos, at the bank and post office in Gibraltar so that any mail to arrive after our departure would be forwarded. We still had a lot of faith in our friends and were sure that once we reached Lagos, we would have ample funds to complete the trip to South Africa. There now remained the small matter of getting to Lagos—across 1,000 miles of desert and three more countries.

We knew that we couldn't possibly drive all the way on our limited finances, but if we could reach Gao, on the Niger River, 1,200 miles south, we could leave the Rover with police and hitch-hike to Lagos, returning with enough money to carry on from there. It seemed to be a reasonable plan, and we were reasonably confident that it would succeed.

PARTING OF THE WAYS

Very few relationships in life are permanent. Many are functional, formed to achieve a certain purpose by combining certain strengths until the goal is attained, and then no longer serve the best interests of either party.

When goals or circumstances change, the players often change as well. New players come on the stage with new roles, and other players leave the stage, to be seen no more.

How many relationships in your life have reached the point where it is time for you, and the other person, to move on?

People are who they are. They are going to do what they are going to do. Each person has his or her own agenda, and you can't change it. Let them go.

SECTION 5:
NEVER GIVE UP

"If at first you don't succeed, try, try again." These words have been responsible for the success of many men and women struggling against apparently insurmountable obstacles.

Sometimes your greatest asset can be your ability to persist longer than the other person. Your willingness to continue even when you feel like quitting will often win you the day.

Between where you are and your goal are a number of hurdles or "tests" that you must successfully pass to succeed. And you never know how many there are. You only know that the number is limited and that at any time you might be just one step away from great achievement.

Expect to meet many obstacles, difficulties, and temporary failures on the way to your goal. They are essential to your eventual success. You need them. They are each sent to teach you something vital that will help you.

And you never can tell how close you are to your goal, right now.

Chapter 17

The Sahara Crossing—
The First Attempt

After leaving Bob at the highway, we returned to town and spent the remainder of the morning rotating our tires, putting the two worst tires on the defective front end. In the heat of midday, we washed all our clothes in the dwindling river, bathed ourselves, and put our things in order for the big push. When the petrol station reopened at 4 p.m., we filled the tank and three jerry cans, and started out on the long haul south.

Welcome to the Sahara

Two hours and 90 kilometers later, only a short distance before Abadla, the first town after Colomb-Béchar, we ran into a sandstorm.

Although it was at least one hour before sundown, the light began to fade rapidly, and the sky seemed overcast. Then, off to the east about five miles, we saw it. Like a huge dirty cloud, thousands of feet high, a wall of murky gray was moving across the land like a monstrous amoeba, enveloping everything in its path. We were driving parallel with its front, and from the wind rattling the plastic windows, we recognized it for what it was immediately.

It seemed to be moving very slowly, and we thought perhaps we'd be able to outrun it. However, its speed was deceptive, and it rolled over us as we reached Abadla. The few people still outside were running for cover, clutching clothes and headdresses over their faces. We didn't stop at all, but continued through the howling, dry blizzard to get out from underneath it. The windows and the air vents were shut tight, but it made little difference; the fine sand swirled in everywhere, and into everything, forcing us to pull our shirts up over our noses to reduce the dust we were inhaling.

The storm was so thick it obscured the road; Geoff had to peer intently through the dusty window to keep us from lurching off into the sagebrush. The wind pummeled at the canvas top and shook the doors angrily, whistling and gusting and thickening, hitting us first from one side and then from the other. Shifting again, it would rise and come straight down the road, shaking the Rover from side to side like a small boat on a choppy sea.

Then, just as suddenly, we were out of it and driving in the quiet sunshine of early evening. Behind us, the whole countryside was blotted out in a whirling mass of gray, while ahead the road flowed on peacefully across the empty landscape. A few kilometers farther, we stopped and wiped the grit from our faces and ears, and dusted off the windows, hearing the distant roar of the storm coming through the still air. We had our first welcome to the Sahara.

I learned that *the storms in life come suddenly and wreak their havoc, causing damage and endangering lives. All you can do is hunker down and hope for the best. And, once the storm is past, to carry on with your life and your journey as best as you can.*

FROM SANDSTORM TO TIRE PROBLEMS

The sun sat on the horizon like a burnished ball of gold when we came out of the sandstorm, then looked like a knife edge of flame. Then it was gone. The darkness fell and then rose again with the twinkling of a million stars. As though on cue, the country had begun to flatten after Abadla, and the occasional mesas that had dwarfed the sagebrushed plain, at heights just under 1,000 feet, ceased to be a feature of the landscape. The headlights sucked in the flowing ribbon of tarmac, to the accompanying purr of the tight little engine and the ominous growl of the scraping tires on the front. The miles fell away into the darkness behind with easy regularity. We drove in silence broken only by the odd comment on how lucky we were that, after all the floundering that had marked our first six weeks on the road, the way ahead at last seemed clear and largely uncomplicated.

There was no traffic, in either direction, for a long time after dark. The first headlights that appeared on the road ahead aroused little interest, until we passed the car and saw that it was on the shoulder and quite stationary. Stopping immediately to investigate, we found an old 1955 Ford packed with seven Arabs among baskets and bedding and one dog. The driver, a bedraggled Algerian in a dirty shirt, got out as we approached and began jabbering rapidly, much too fast for us to understand.

We answered him in English and got the desired reaction—he shut up. Then, speaking slowly and distinctly in French, we gleaned that he had stopped for some reason, after which the car had refused to start again. Bringing the torch from the Rover, we lifted the hood, exposing a filthy engine with jumbles of loose wires and broken fittings—a real mechanic's nightmare. With a pair of pliers and a screwdriver, we tightened everything that had any thread left and told him to give it a try. It made no difference; the engine turned over but would not fire.

There was no question about leaving them. In that empty country, the code of the road required that we either send them on their way or take them. I brought the Rover around and Geoff, over the protests of the Arab, took the wheel of the Ford while I pushed the old wreck down the highway. After a quarter of a mile, it finally caught with a roar, sputtering and coughing. Shouting over the noise of the engine, we told him to keep the revs up and, no matter what, not to stop before Abadla. We waited until the rumble of the old Ford had faded into the distance before continuing. It had been our first opportunity to reciprocate the assistance we had received, and we were glad of it.

Half an hour later, we came upon another vehicle and were met with a strange scene. A half-ton Citroen pickup truck, piled high with baskets and blankets, was parked by the road, while behind it on the ground, 16 Arabs squatted peacefully around a little fire. Stopping the Rover where we could watch it, we approached and inquired of the man who rose to greet us if he wasn't in need of anything.

Oh yes, he said easily, he was out of petrol and would be most pleased to buy a little from us, if we had enough to spare. But first, he said, we must have a cup of tea. Always suspicious of smiling foreigners, and more so in the middle of the night, we declined the tea but poured 10 liters of petrol into his tank, charging him what it had cost us in Colomb-Béchar. However, he was not to be put off, and insisted we come and sit by the fire.

An old Arab was feeding pieces of broken brushwood into the little blaze under a blackened pot, and everyone seemed quite merry about being stuck in the middle of nowhere, 40 miles from the nearest town. The driver produced a package of cigarettes and we squatted with the fellows to join the party. When the tea was ready, we relaxed a little and became a part of the gang.

The tea was poured into thick, little clay cups, and was sweet, minty, and very hot. Soon we were chatting away jovially. But for us the complete nonchalance of the strange group toward their circumstances was slightly unfathomable. We were enjoying the tea and the chatter but were becoming uncomfortable about the time we were losing, whereas they didn't seem to care at all.

Finally, the tea was finished and the party broke up. All 16 of the long-robed Arabs arose to shake our hands, some twice, with cheery smiles and vigorous head nodding. As we regained our vehicle, they began to reload themselves back into the pickup, until it was a mass of humanity, the rear end almost touching the ground from the heavy burden. We waited until they continued on their way before driving on. We were behind on our schedule, and hoped our services wouldn't be required anymore that night.

About 20 minutes later, our left front tire went flat with a dull plop. In the 135 kilometers from Béchar, the half-worn tire had been ground right down to the tube and was ruined completely. The other front tire was only slightly better.

We realized that we were faced with a major mechanical problem, and although we had a spare tire of sorts, it would be folly to continue. We drove the vehicle 20 yards off the road, parked it, and went to sleep on the sand nearby.

We had left civilization behind, but we hadn't left the flies. More dependable than an alarm clock, they drove us out of our bags at half past sunrise, buzzing delightedly at the two guests who had stopped during the night. A sober inspection of the Rover showed that it would have to be partially repaired before we moved, or the other tires would likely be destroyed, leaving us stranded. Mounting the front bumper on the jerry cans as before, we dug out under the wheels with the machetes and removed them to see what we could see. And all that we could see was the other side of the front wheels. We decided against dismantling anything before having a qualified opinion on the cause of the trouble. I departed for Béchar, hitchhiking, half an hour later.

It was one hour before a car came along the lonely road northbound, another hour before I reached Abadla, and three hours after that when I was dropped off in Béchar. In the meantime, the sun had burned off the coolness of morning and set in like a bake oven, making me very thankful that I'd thought to bring a canteen. The lack of passing motorists had turned an 80-mile trip into a five-hour ordeal in the hot, empty land.

At the main garage in Béchar, I tried to explain our problem. They told me that they would have to see the vehicle before passing judgment. I next tried the Foreign Legion post on the edge of town, but they wouldn't let me in the gate to speak to a mechanic. The guard, however, told me to ask at the Highway Department building, a mile down the road.

The girl at the desk in the entrance hall ushered me into the unadorned office of Monsieur Leroux, the type of man who can be found occasionally in obscure places, seemingly for the set purpose of restoring one's faith in human nature. He was a husky man with a long face and an ability to grasp the essentials of a situation, no matter how confused its presentation, and my presentation was surely confused.

As soon as I had outlined the problem and showed him approximately where the vehicle was on the large wall map, he told me to go back to the Rover. He would radio to his garage in Beni-Abbes, 40 kilometers past the spot, and have someone sent out to take a look at it. There was no question of payment, or mention of the fact that it wasn't his responsibility to help itinerant travelers, nor would he accept any thanks. Only 10 minutes after entering the building, I was back on the road, waiting for the next car south.

Four hours later, I finally grinned down a truck that got me back to Abadla, where I waited another two hours for a second ride in another truck, arriving back at the Land Rover just before sunset.

It was like coming home after a weekend out of town. Geoff had passed the day reading and waving to the few motorists, all of whom had stopped to offer assistance, food, and water before going on. Two hours previously, he said, a light truck had come from the south, and the two Arabs inside had stopped to inspect the Land Rover before saying something about tomorrow morning and disappearing back down the road.

I explained what had taken place in Béchar with Monsieur Leroux, from which we reasoned that the two fellows had been sent and would return in the morning to repair the defect. We were there for another night.

TIME FOR A COUNCIL MEETING

It was time for another war council to decide how to proceed from that point. The mechanical difficulties were only part of the problem facing us, since we needed a minimum of two new tires before we could continue toward Lagos. The repairs were going to be expensive, we reckoned, and in our financial position, we couldn't have them done and continue with the Rover, too. Since going back, as Bob had done, was unthinkable, we would have to find another solution.

There was only one alternative—hitchhike to Lagos, pick up the money, and hitchhike back for the vehicle. It would be extremely difficult, we knew, but it was our only choice. We certainly could not quit, not at that stage of the game.

We could leave our Land Rover at the Highway Department in Colomb-Béchar, load up with enough food for two weeks, and hope for the best. Once over the Sahara, which increasingly seemed to be our big stumbling block, we would be in more heavily populated countries, and would surely get along somehow. Realizing that any more discussion was worse than fruitless, we turned in early to be well-rested for the coming day.

At 7 a.m., the light truck from the previous afternoon reappeared, and the two Arabs examined the Rover once more. The driver of the vehicle shrugged and said that there was nothing he could do, but he would escort us back to Abadla, to the workshop, and perhaps they could repair it.

We put the old spare on in place of the ruined tire and followed him slowly. The mechanic at Abadla hemmed and hawed for the entire morning before informing us that he knew nothing about Land Rovers and we would have to go to Béchar to find someone who did. He had held back that little tidbit of information until it was too hot to drive, forcing us to wait the afternoon in a little mud-walled café, listening to the wailing of Arab music coming from the speaker above the door.

The return to Béchar took four hours of 15-mile-per-hour driving, and it was with great relief that we made it back to the riverbank to spend another night. It was a bit like Dunquerque, we felt, in that we had made a successful retreat, but we weren't any closer to winning the war.

We woke in the morning amid a herd of goats bleating, their bells tinkling merrily. The old gaffer steering them along the river-bank showed no emotion at the rudeness of our awakening, aside from a toothless grin, and plodded on, swinging his staff. Fortunately, the goats avoided stepping on us directly, and we withdrew into our sleeping bags to avoid any low-flying hooves until they were past. No one sleeps after something like that, not us anyway, even if the flies weren't there to remind us that it was time to be up and out hitchhiking.

Our patron saint of Colomb-Béchar, Monsieur Leroux, readily agreed to our leaving the vehicle in the Highway Department compound, where it could be watched during the day. We thanked him profusely once more, then pulled on our loaded rucksacks and hiked out to the main highway.

Attacking to the Rear

Sometimes a tactical retreat, allowing time to reassess and reconsolidate, can save the entire situation. There is a time to advance boldly, and there is a time to back off and reconsider.

The person who is going back the fastest is often the person who is going forward the fastest in the long run.

Conserve your resources. There are some decisions you cannot afford to make. The cost of being wrong is too high.

Look at your life today. What are the major sources of stress in your world? In what areas should you withdraw and regroup?

Taking time to rethink and reevaluate your situation can enable you to see it in a much better light.

CHAPTER 18

THE SAHARA CROSSING—
THE SECOND ATTEMPT

Looking back at it with a shudder, I can think of no pastime more unrewarding and more fraught with disappointment than that of a hitchhiker in Algeria, North Africa. A more miserable, wretched, soul-searching way of traveling surely cannot exist. With temperatures during the day climbing over 120 degrees Fahrenheit and not a breath of wind stirring, with distances between towns of 50 miles or more, and with almost no traffic on the roads, except for a brief period each morning and afternoon, traveling by thumb has to be the lowest form of mobility.

We got our first ride just after 10 a.m., and 10 minutes later it ended at a small village on the outskirts of town. And there we sat, for five long, hot, broiling hours in the raging sun. The urchins from the nearby village threw stones at us for a while, and then ran away laughing. However, we tired of the game before they did and our aim was better, so they eventually left us alone to fry in peace. Our real enemy was the sun—that merciless ball of flame, producing a heat we didn't think was possible, coming as we did from the cool mountain country of British Columbia.

Not only was such heat possible, but it was very real, and in our circumstances unavoidable. There was very little traffic on the road, so we couldn't seek shade without risking missing a possible ride. Although we weren't having much luck with our schedules, we were still determined to get to our destination as quickly as possible, in spite of the difficulties it entailed. The heat, as terrible as it was, we accepted as an occupational hazard, to be endured if it was a part of the job of world-beating.

At 4 p.m. we finally got our second ride, in the back of a vegetable truck loaded with onions, oranges, and Arabs. We were so pleased to be under way again that we would have ridden in a garbage truck.

When the Arabs started singing a native refrain, we joined in and howled along happily. While they were laughing among themselves at us, we were stealing all the oranges we could without being seen, stuffing them into our already fat rucksacks. The driver turned off in Abadla, stopping to let us climb out. But as we started hiking away, he suddenly called us back. Going to the rear of the truck, he pulled out a sack and gave us each four oranges, smiling and wishing us "Bon voyage" at the same time. We thanked him humbly and walked away, feeling like fools for stealing a few oranges earlier.

Lugging our packs to the dry riverbed on the far side of Abadla, once more we sat morosely and waited by the roadside. It was dusk before a Frenchman stopped and took us another five kilometers, turning off on a small dirt road and leaving us far from any human habitation just as night fell.

Hours later, another car came by and stopped. The Arab in the small, overloaded Citroen station wagon insisted that he had plenty of room for us. We didn't need much encouragement, but the Arab was wrong; among the family, the baskets, and the bundles, he did not have room for us. Nonetheless, we squeezed in, and he talked at us incessantly.

During the next two hours, from our cramped positions in the rear seat, we vigorously agreed with him that: a) Arabic was the most important language in the world; b) that his skinny daughter had a beautiful voice; and c) everyone should see Algeria before they die.

At midnight, he let us off at the turning point to Beni-Abbes. A tiny two-room house stood at the lonely crossroads, and for some reason, the Algerian police were checking identification papers there by lantern light. We had to stand for half an hour with several truck drivers before showing our passports to the bored policeman. We then shouldered our packs and walked down the road for 15 minutes, under the silent, star-riddled desert sky. By the quiet roadside, we spread our bags and drifted gratefully off to sleep.

We had been on the road for 14 hours, covering the impressive distance of 140 miles, and the traffic on the road was diminishing with every mile we proceeded south into the desert. At the rate we were going, it would be a long, long way to Tipperary.

To Hell with Hitchhiking

The decrease in vegetation was the first thing we noticed in the morning, after the flies had arrived to tell us that the sun was up. The ground was bare, rocky gravel, flat and unbroken for miles, and the road stretched across it north to south, from horizon to horizon. The tiny building at the crossroads looked like a toy block that had been left behind when the desert floor was swept clean, and we felt like tiny ants in a huge, empty ballroom.

In the five hours between our waking that morning and the sun reaching its zenith, only three trucks passed on the road south. Each driver stopped and inquired about our destination, but since they were not going too far, they all told us to wait for another truck going farther.

By 11 a.m. the heat was too intense for us to sit unprotected any longer, hotter still than the day before, and since there had been no traffic for the last two hours, we donned our packs and hiked back to the little white building, to stay until the sun abated somewhat.

The hike was only about one mile, but it felt like five miles. We were sweating and puffing with the effort when we flopped down on the bench on the cement verandah. The building turned out to be a café of sorts, selling as its sole product warm orange soda to passing drivers. The owner was definitely not in the business to get rich.

By noon, several Arabs—two boys, four young men, and three grizzled older fellows—wandered in from somewhere to sit out the heat. They were soon joined by a young, clear-eyed Algerian who parked his truck by the road and lazily sat down with a magazine at the one table on the porch. We were there for the afternoon with nothing to do, so we eventually started chatting with the amiable driver, who immediately offered us a ride back north to Colomb-Béchar if we were going that way.

We declined, but as the sun burned hotter and hotter, we began to rethink the whole idea of hitchhiking.

"Geoff, this is the stupidest thing we've ever done," I said.

Outside the building, the rising heat waves were so heavy they blurred everything over a distance of 100 yards. Even in the shade we were breathing laboriously, the salty perspiration dripping off our chins and soaking through our clothes. The air was heavy with the drone of the ever-present flies.

"What else can we do?" he replied after a while.

"I don't know, but there has to be another solution. It's so stinking hot here that you could can the heat and take it home."

"In the last two days we have traveled only 140 miles. Do you know how many days we could be stuck in the desert?"

We sat musing quietly for a few minutes.

"We need more money; we'll have to borrow some more. Is there a Canadian embassy in Algiers?"

"There's only one way to find out. You speak better French than I do. Tell your friend we accept his offer for a ride."

That afternoon in the oppressive heat, we worked out a new strategy, rationalizing away the idea of hitchhiking with reasons that were as good as they were obvious. The energy-sapping, 120-degree heat was making itself felt, and it was difficult to envision glorious sagas of winning in the face of great odds when we were feeling like boiled dishrags. *There comes a point when stubborn resolve gives over to simple reasoning, and we were there.*

We needed our vehicle to make the trip, and we needed a way to have our vehicle running properly. We would return to Béchar that night with the truck driver, and tomorrow Geoff would leave for Algiers with a hard-luck story to deliver to the Canadian embassy, about how we had mailed most of our money to Lagos, and due to unforeseen difficulties, needed a small loan to get us there. We would promise to repay the Canadian representative immediately upon our arrival. In the meantime, I would remain in Colomb-Béchar to sell our extra groceries, raise some money, and enact the necessary repairs. It was a good plan, we figured, and much more logical than this heart-breaking, death-defying hitchhiking.

LUNCH FOR EVERYONE

Borrowing the proprietor's stove about 3 p.m., we got out a can of beans and started preparing a late lunch, with every Arab eye on the porch following our movements. Up to then, they had been sitting quietly in various positions of lassitude on the floor and along the bench at the end of the porch, saying nothing, doing nothing, just sitting blankly. None of them had anything to eat, and from the ragged clothes that hung on them, young and old alike, the reason was obvious. Missing a meal wasn't going to be a new experience for them.

"Geoff, I can think of a better idea than dragging all this food back to Béchar," I said, referring to the bulky packs.

He looked at the blank stares coming from the hungry Arabs, and then back at the packs.

"Yeah," he said. "These are the only people I know who are worse off than we are."

Borrowing a large pot from the wall of the café, we emptied 10 cans of beans and spaghetti into it. The unkempt proprietor, who lived in one room and sold his wares from the other, watched us thoughtfully for a while, knowing what we were doing without our having to explain it. He had been ignoring the presence of the ragged crew on the porch, preferring to do what little business he was doing with cash customers—the truck driver, Geoff, and myself being the only ones there with money. Now he felt that he had better get into the act, perhaps fearing that he would lose face if foreigners fed his people.

As the stew began to steam and boil, he produced a huge loaf of bread and a few tin plates, which he laid out on the slatted table. He helped us to ladle the stew and pass the plates to everyone, the gang squatting on their haunches, eating two to a plate, slurping the food down and jabbering happily in Arabic the whole time. The proprietor didn't partake, but brought us another bottle of orange soda, a gift this time, and sat watching interestedly while we ate. Because of the language barrier, the preparation and serving had been done with a minimum of conversation, but the communication seemed to be quite good for all that.

I've learned in life that you will regret many things, but you'll never regret being too kind or too fair. You'll never regret being too helpful or too generous. Of those to whom much is given, much is expected. Never be reluctant to give of yourself and your substance. It always comes back to you.

BACK TO BÉCHAR

The ride back to Béchar was broken at Abadla (a town we were rather sick of seeing) while the driver chatted with a couple of his friends. We sat in the truck the whole time, muttering, but knowing that we were better off waiting impatiently in the truck than waiting warily along that empty highway. At sunset back in Colomb-Béchar, we straggled up the stony riverbed to the palm grove to spend our sixth night in Algeria. Except that the riverbed was now dry, things were pretty much the same as they had been the evening of our arrival a few days ago.

The two days of exposure to the unmitigated heat exacted their toll that night. Geoff was lucky—he only paid in physical exhaustion and was unconscious shortly after dark, sleeping through the night without stirring. I know he didn't stir because I was awake with stomach cramps and dysentery until the early hours of the morning.

For the rest of the time we traveled in Africa, the dysentery (otherwise referred to as the Algerian runs, the Nigerian trots, tummy palaver, rumbling guts) was a part of life. It was brought on by the weather, the water, the insects, or the local foods, but it was ever-present. *Constipation* is a word that does not exist and is not understood in Africa above the tropic of Capricorn, or below, for that matter.

With four cans of spaghetti, two cans of beans, and 10 dinars in his pocket, Geoff took all the papers he would need to prove his story to the consulate in Algiers and left the next morning, expecting to be back within three days. I wished him luck and waved him a good-bye. He was on his way to do his job, and I was hiking back to the Highway Department to start my job.

In the rear of the little bungalow housing the Highway Department were situated a bath and two small bedrooms, one of which the radio operators offered me as a place to stay until Geoff returned. The offer was accepted immediately; I had already been wondering how I was going to keep our things together and out of the hands of the many wandering, light-fingered Arabs while the vehicle was being repaired.

After moving our things into the room, I sorted out enough food for 12 days and then took the remainder, except for six cans of beans and spaghetti, into town to sell.

Scanning the shelves of the little store for the prices of similar articles to those I had to sell, I added the sum, tacked on 20 percent, and then started the bartering. The Arab storekeeper was not a beginner at this game. He also worked out the value of my things—mostly peas, condensed milk, beans and spaghetti—added it up on a piece of paper, divided it by four, and made me a "final" offer. Twenty minutes of final offers and ultimatums later, we came to a compromise at about 60 percent of the retail value, 104 dinars, or about $24, approximately what we had paid for the items in Gibraltar.

The finances replenished somewhat, I then took the Rover into the main garage in Béchar, where I explained our hitting the bump to the jovial manager in the service department. He would have to take it apart and look at it. "Come back tomorrow after lunch," he said.

We seemed to be making a little progress, I thought. I certainly hoped it wouldn't cost more than the $40 that represented our total balance. There was no telling how successful Geoff would be with his story in Algiers, and it would be a tragic thing for him to come back broke, find me also broke, and the Land Rover in the shop with an account against it. That would be too much.

Two days later the Rover was finally returned to me. One steering rod had been bent, shortening the distance between the forward edges of the front tires and causing the excessive wear. After discovering the fault, the mechanics took it out, heated it with an acetylene torch, tapped it straight, and reinstalled it. From beginning to end, once they got at it, the job took half an hour, involved no new parts, and cost a total of 12 dinars, about $2.50.

For the two days I had been waiting, nervously fingering the 180 dinars in my pocket, I had been trying to think of something else to sell just in case I didn't have enough money. We had ruined three tires, been set back 10 days already, lost a childhood friend, and suffered the heat of two days in the open—all for a lousy 12-dinar repair job. Driving the snug-steering vehicle back to the radio shack, I was trying to decide whether I was mad, glad, or sad—or a bit of all three, and how much of each.

I learned later that *often the most important thing you can do when faced with a new problem or situation is to stop and think for a while. Don't rely on your own limited knowledge. Ask someone for input, advice or guidance. Sometimes a few words or instructions from an experienced person can save you huge expenditures of time or money.*

The next problem on the agenda was tires. Although the garage had no new tires for a Land Rover, it had one good used tire, which I bought for 50 dinars. A search of the junkyards around Béchar turned up nothing, but in back of the Highway Department, half buried in the sand, was the remains of a Land Rover that had been demolished in a collision. The tires had blown out on impact, but except for tears in the sidewalls, two of them were almost new.

The parts department of the garage denied having what I needed, but the thin-faced, harried Arab agreed to look anyway, and he found them—large rubber patches made for the inside of tires. These patches are frowned upon universally by companies dealing in tires, for obvious reasons. But, I had once had occasion to use them on a car when I was in school, and I knew they had amazing potential.

After three hours of scraping, sanding, and shaping—and after buying two new, heavy-duty tubes—I now had four good tires and a spare, and the Land Rover was ready to roll.

Adding to the delight of having the Rover repaired at such a low cost, a Frenchman, with whom I had chatted at the garage, came by at that moment and said that he had a sixth tire for me if I wanted it. He rolled it out of his carport and showed me that it was ripped on one side, but if I could use it, I could have it.

From various inquiries among the truck drivers in Béchar, as well as a bit of advice from the garage owner and the friendly Frenchman, I learned that there was an 800-mile stretch in the desert where it would be impossible to get petrol or any repairs. The trucks that went across in convoys, every two weeks or so, carried half a dozen spare tires, spare parts enough to overhaul their entire vehicles, and enough petrol for the trip both ways. They said that the desert was dotted with the abandoned vehicles of travelers who had not been properly equipped. This "simple" matter of a long, hot drive was turning out to be a very complex affair indeed.

The evening after settling the tire problem, I removed a 16-gallon tank from a ruined truck and mounted it on blocks in the back of the Rover. That gave us a fuel capacity of 39 gallons; I figured at 25 miles per gallon that was seven gallons more than we would need for the long stretch. With the addition of a jack, we were as prepared as we could possibly be for the crossing. All I needed now was Geoff and a little bit of money, and Geoff was already one day overdue.

THE FAMILIAR WORK OF WAITING

Geoff had reckoned on covering the 500 miles to Algiers in one day, allotting one day to obtain the money and one more day for the trip back. He had hoped to arrive the night of the third day, or at the latest, the morning of the fourth. Before being given the place to stay at the Highway Department, I had assured him that I would camp by the riverbed on the edge of town and be waiting for him when he returned. The vehicle now being road ready, I therefore started making regular pilgrimages to the riverbank, where I would sit and read *Paris Match*, looking up the new French words to pass the time.

The time began to drag after the fourth day and the fifth, and the sixth came and went with no sign of him. I read or wrote poetry, and went for walks. I gave the young radio operator a couple of driving lessons, and started going into town with him at lunchtime to eat Arab food. I did calisthenics to keep fit. I wandered around the town. I wrote in my journal and translated bits of French. But still the time dragged and I began to worry. What if Geoff had been hurt or fallen sick, and was unable to remember that I was back in Béchar? He had the passports and all the papers from the Rover, so I couldn't leave and go looking for him without being arrested for lack of identification.

I checked at the post office to see if he'd written, but there was nothing. On the morning of the seventh day, I drove to the riverbank again and waited until noon, but there was still no sign of him. More than impatient, I was genuinely concerned, nervous, and worried.

A FOOLISH ERROR

That afternoon, when the traffic on the roads had stopped for the midday heat, I did a very foolish thing. Thinking perhaps that a bit of strenuous exercise would relieve the tension, I went for a long walk in the open country west of town, bareheaded, in the very heat of the day.

Half an hour of walking in the broiling sun brought me to a place where thousands of empty bottles had been dumped in piles over an area of several acres. Setting a long row of bottles on a ridge, I walked back a few yards and hurled rocks at them until my arm was sore. Feeling a bit giddy from the 120-degree heat, I walked back to my "home" an hour later.

The radio operator on duty, an ex-soldier, looked up when I came in and commented that it was not a good idea to walk around without a hat in the sun. I laughed and told him that Canadians were hardy—we didn't worry too much about such things. He left at 6 p.m. as usual, and after one more visit to the riverbank, I crawled onto my canvas mat and went to sleep. For some reason I was feeling especially tired.

The next morning I couldn't get up. The noise of the radio operators arriving in the room outside the door woke me, as it had done for the previous week, but my body failed to respond when I tried to stand. "Perhaps I need more sleep," I thought, and closed my eyes once more. It seemed only a moment later that I reopened them, but the sun was leaking in the window from high in the sky. My watch said 11:30, making a total of 15 hours since I had laid down the night before.

"This is ridiculous," I mused. "No one needs that much sleep." With a deep breath and a shove, I got to my feet. That did it. A searing pain shot through my head and down the length of my body, like a tongue of flame, and everything went black, with flashing lights dancing and screaming through my eyeballs. Lurching against the wall, I just stood there shaking in agony, my limbs trembling and my heart pounding insanely. "What the hell is wrong with me?" I thought, as the pain lashed across the nerve endings. I'd never believed such suffering to be possible.

For five minutes I remained perfectly still, and gradually the room came back into focus, the roar of blood in my temples abating slowly. I had to get to the bathroom outside the door, I thought. I must be poisoned from that Arab food I've been eating. That's why my abdomen felt like a knife was being twisted into the muscle. Moving very slowly, I aimed a foot in the direction of the door six feet away, and pushed from the wall gently, any way toward it. The crescendo of pain crashed back, worse than before, leaving me gripping the door handle from the floor, holding on for dear life while the cold sweat dribbled down my face.

It was another five minutes before the furious pounding diminished again, and another 20 minutes before I was able to reach the bathroom on my knees and get back to the canvas on the floor. I collapsed, unconscious, thoroughly spent with exertion and confirmed in the belief that I could soon be dead. I think I might have been looking forward to the relief of it.

For the next two days, I was in a state of semiconsciousness. My existence consisted of trips to the bathroom, aspirins washed down with the water from the canteen, and dazed slumber. I found that if I didn't move a muscle, my head remained clear. The Arab radio operators accepted that I was sick with something, and paid no more attention to me, except for the young fellow, who plagued me with questions and requests for driving lessons, to which I was barely able to reply. Once it began to appear as though I would live after all, I discarded the idea of seeking medical attention because of the possible cost. Those were very grim days indeed.

On the afternoon of the third day of illness, I was able to get up and move around, and though still weak, drove out to the riverbank to check for Geoff. That evening, I drank a little tea with plenty of milk and once more collapsed to sleep for 12 hours. What I had was a "minor" case of sunstroke. This bit of bad luck I experienced, through foolishness and ignorance, serves as an excellent example of just how hot it really is in that country. And we still had several hundred miles to go before we would arrive in the hottest part.

One of your greatest enemies, or weaknesses, can be complacency. Never take an important situation for granted. Never assume that things will be all right whether you do anything or not. Be careful.

On the fourth day of illness, the pain and the constriction in my stomach were gone, replaced by a nagging hunger, reminding me that it had been a long time since I'd eaten. After checking to see if Geoff had returned, I bought six eggs in town and took them back to the radio shack to scramble. The eggs were just beginning to steam when the stillness was shattered by a loud whoop coming from a dirty, unshaved, rucksacked fellow wearing a battered old straw hat.

BACK IN BUSINESS

It was Geoff in all his glory. He was weather-beaten, dusty, and eight days late, but from the smile on his face, I knew right away that he had the money.

It had not been easy to get rides. Rides on the main road north, when there had been traffic, were easy to come by, but there had not been a lot of traffic going long distances. In the course of eight rides—after being detoured and lost—Geoff had spent almost two days on the way to Algiers, arriving there late in the afternoon of the second day. By the time he made his way to the part of town housing the foreign embassies, not only were they all closed, but also, there was no Canadian delegation to be found.

Sitting down on the curb opposite the heavily guarded palace of President Ben Bella with a can of beans, Geoff pried it open with a screwdriver, using the bent tin lid as a spoon to wolf down the contents. He was debating with himself over where he could sleep the night when a well-muscled, sharply-dressed Algerian in tight black pants and a purple T-shirt walked past him on the sidewalk, stopped, then turned around and came back.

Curiously but in a friendly manner, the Algerian asked Geoff where he was from and where he was going with a rucksack on his back. Hunched over the can of beans, Geoff replied that he had just arrived from Colomb-Béchar, and was going to visit his embassy in the morning. When asked where he was staying in Algiers, Geoff replied that a temporary lack of funds was limiting his choices; he was going to sleep in a park. The good-looking Algerian laughed and said that Geoff could sleep in his nearby apartment if he wished. A bit suspicious but game for anything, Geoff thanked him for the offer and accompanied the Algerian home.

Although not large, the apartment was in a new building and quite luxuriously furnished, with a balcony overlooking a nearby hospital. Once inside, the Algerian poured them both drinks from a small bar, later frying a couple of steaks in the kitchenette, and kept up a steady stream of questions and jokes for several hours. Geoff was becoming sleepier as the evening progressed, and a bit uncomfortable after noticing that there didn't seem to be a bed in the apartment, let alone two beds.

Just after 10 p.m. the friendly Algerian indicated that it was late and time for Geoff to sleep. Turning a handle on one of the walls, he pulled down a well-concealed double bed and told Geoff to make himself comfortable.

"No," said Geoff, "you sleep here; I'll sleep on the floor."

"No, no," said the Algerian, smiling. "You must sleep in the bed."

"No thank you," said Geoff, also smiling. "The floor would be just fine; I much prefer sleeping on floors anyway."

The Algerian insisted and Geoff resisted, beginning to think he'd better go and find a park after all.

The Algerian looked at Geoff perplexedly, then broke into a big grin. Motioning for him to follow, he led him to the balcony and pointed to the hospital below. "That is where I work," he said, "and I am leaving for work now. I won't be back until the morning."

Geoff would be alone in the apartment, and he was free to sleep wherever he chose. Geoff was already in the bed when the fellow left 10 minutes later.

Early the next morning, Geoff put on his clean shirt, carried from Béchar in a plastic bag, and went to peddle his story. The victim was the British consul, on the third floor of an office building downtown.

The consul was singularly unmoved by the tale of woe, and the array of papers proving the existence of a vehicle and a destitute friend in the desert. Every summer, he said, people like Geoff came there looking for handouts or passage money home. "We are not authorized to supply funds, except in the case of emergency or theft," he went on, explaining that even then it was only the necessary amount to fly the destitute traveler back to England. "Haven't you got any relatives to whom you can wire for money?" he asked.

Geoff replied that he could ask his parents, but he couldn't afford a cable (all the money was in Lagos, you see). "Well, old boy," the consul replied brightly, "you can use our wire service, and pay for it when the money comes." He wrote out a request for $150, which the consul sent that morning. After writing a letter explaining the circumstances behind the request and mailing it, Geoff shouldered his rucksack and wandered into the streets to begin the wait.

After two days of sleeping in a urine-stained alley while the rats nibbled at his ankles and ate the bits of bread in his rucksack, Geoff began to think that there had to be a better place to sleep. An undersecretary at the consulate, where he hung around most of the day waiting for a reply to his cable, told him of an old hotel on the waterfront run by an Englishman for seamen and expatriates. The manager of the Republican Hotel listened to his tale of desert tragedy, and told him he could sleep in the broom closet if he wished. After the alley, the broom closet was just dandy.

For the next five days, Geoff haunted the British consulate, stopping to inquire every two hours. The rest of the time he spent reading old periodicals and anything available concerning the country where we were going, finding out many interesting details that were to become very important later.

And if I wasn't exactly enjoying my sojourn in Béchar, Geoff was a long way from delighting in the excitement of Algiers. Having no way of knowing how I was faring, and thus feeling obligated to keep expenses down to a minimum, he refused the consul's offer of a small loan, instead living for the entire 10 days on his limited supply of canned food and the 10 dinars he had taken with him.

On the morning of the ninth day after leaving Béchar, a bank draft came through the consulate in the name of Geoffrey E. Laundy for the amount of $150. Half an hour after receiving it, he was on his way out of town, on the southbound road.

A good night's sleep in a culvert did him no harm, and neither did a ride straight through to Béchar early the next morning. When there was no sign of me at the riverbank, except for a lot of tracks,

Geoff went to the only other place he could think of me being—the Highway Department. There I was.

That afternoon, when the petrol station reopened, we filled the tank and the jerry cans and once more drove out of Béchar toward the south. After 17 days in, out, and around that town, we never wanted to see it again. But without those 17 days, the alterations to the vehicle, and the lift to our fortitude and finances, I do not like to think of the things we might never have seen again, or at all.

THANK YOUR LUCKY STARS

These were the worst of times, and simultaneously, the best of times. We were frustrated and stymied at every turn. But unbeknownst to us, we were learning at a rapid rate. We were becoming the kind of people we would need to be for the crossing ahead.

Every experience in your life is being orchestrated to teach you something you need to know to move forward. Often when you are in the midst of a crisis, you can't make out the lesson. But it's there nonetheless.

Give thanks for all the good things in your life. Actively seek out the blessings in the most difficult of circumstances, and the good in the most aggravating of people.

The more you give thanks for what you have, the more things you will have to be thankful for.

CHAPTER 19

THIRD TIME LUCKY

We were in no real hurry that evening, all the desire to rush having drained away in the aftermath of almost three weeks of going nowhere, except perhaps growing a bit older and wiser. We both had time to think over what we were doing, to examine the idea as a whole, and we chatted quietly, philosophically, as the miles rolled steadily by, to the comforting hum of good tires on good road.

Geoff brought an article from a *Life* magazine on existentialism, which he read as we drove, and after he had folded it and put it away, we discussed the theory of "engagement," the coming to grips with your environment, preceding "essence," the maximum enjoyment and satisfaction possible in life. We agreed that since we left Vancouver, we had been more involved with the business of actually asserting ourselves in our environment than ever before in our lives, and increasingly so since we left London seven weeks previously. It had been damn difficult much of the time, in fact, but we couldn't think of anything we'd rather be doing than driving that little green Land Rover down that quiet road, toward the heart of the greatest wasteland on earth, with the stars twinkling overhead and a song in our hearts. If that was existentialism, we believed in it.

Once more through Abadla and across the dry riverbed, down past where we had come to an inglorious halt 17 days before, through the crossroads at Beni-Abbes, which had been our furthest point south, and on into the night we drove, not sleeping until we were far away from the spots in the unfeeling desert that had marked our defeats. Our destination was Adrar, a tiny dot 376 miles south of Colomb-Béchar. From Adrar, it was 86 miles to Reggane, an even smaller dot, and then came the 800-mile stretch to Gao. At midnight we stopped for our meatballs and spaghetti, washed down with black coffee to clear the drowsiness for the all-night drive.

The map indicated that the paved road ended 100 miles north of Adrar, and when we reached that point, there was no need to check to be sure. The Rover lurched at an angle, straightened, slammed into a series of ruts that almost tore the wheel out of my hands, bounced crazily, and shook to a halt, my foot hard on the brake.

A brief inspection showed that we were still on the road, what there was of it, and that we would need to creep along at 10 miles per hour for five hours until the sun came up the next morning. But with the rise of the orange-gold ball far to the east, it was not the road that arrested our attention.

We were just then atop the last rise in a series of low rocky hills, overlooking the desert floor, which stretched away forever, the distant horizon obscured by a pink haze. Silently, reverently almost, Geoff stopped the vehicle. We climbed onto a jagged shelf to take a good look, gazing in quiet amazement.

THE FACE OF DEATH

Before us flowed a ragged landscape, silent as a graveyard, and beyond a few tufts of withered grass. The Sahara seemed to be waiting angrily, without a sound or the slightest trace of movement, like a monstrous trap for us to step into. We stood staring at the immensity of what we had dared to challenge in a half-broken vehicle with three bald tires and enough gasoline to get halfway across. The lifeless vastitude of the desert, and the terrible ignorance in which we had looked upon it as "just something in the way," gave me a feeling of looking in the face of death.

We realized clearly that *if we had not had every difficulty of the last 17 days and learned the appropriate lessons, we would certainly have "died in the desert."*

About 30 miles before Adrar, when the sun was high in the sky and the midday heat was building up, we stopped by the track to sleep the day in a conical mud hut. It was deserted, and had been for some time, judging by the amount of sand that had drifted into it. For our purposes, it was ideal. The flies made sound sleep impossible, but we managed to doze comfortably until 3 p.m., when we ate "breakfast" and refilled the tank from the jerry cans before continuing into the town. We had finally curbed our tendency to rush things, and against the timelessness of that huge wasteland, we would have felt a little foolish going any faster than was absolutely necessary.

The drab brown buildings of the spread-out Arab town of Adrar began merging from the haze of dust and heat about 15 minutes before we arrived. It was supposed to have 1,000 inhabitants, but the town was sprawled over several miles with no main center of population. A huge empty lot, probably at one time a parade ground for the French army, marked the point from which the wide, dusty streets meandered in all directions toward the outskirts. The one trace of "the good life" facing this square was an old hotel, for which we aimed. One day in the heat of the desert—and though it was early evening, it was still hot—makes a person rather favorably inclined toward something cold to drink when the opportunity presents itself—and that hotel reeked of opportunity.

NEWS OF A CONVOY

As we got out of the vehicle, a European (with short khaki pants, thin white legs, knobby knees, bald head, red face, and sunburned arms) approached us and asked us in heavily accented English if we were also going with the convoy. "What convoy?" we asked.

We knew of the occasional truck convoys formed for mutual security on the journey to Mali, but they were largely suspended during the summer months because of the increase in temperature. He accompanied us into the hotel and explained.

This was a late convoy, and the last of the season, which had been forming for 10 days and now consisted of almost 30 trucks. They would be leaving the next day, or at the latest, the day after— a rare stroke of luck for us indeed. Now that we were getting into this desert-crossing business, the prospect of 800 miles alone was not a joyous one, and the existence of the convoy, which we had not suspected, was a fact we viewed with no little relief.

I later learned that there is strength in numbers—as long as all the players are unified behind a common vision and goal and everyone is committed to pulling their own weight. Real strength lies in unity.

The fellow who gave us this information, Hermann, was a German from Hamburg, and was also a minister with a degree in theology. He told us that he was on a leave of absence from his parish, hitchhiking down through Africa to study the need of the black people for Christianity and to write a thesis to be applied toward his doctorate. He spoke French as well as English, and we were rather impressed. We even stopped swearing for a few minutes.

Hermann had arranged a ride with some other Germans as far as Gao, 800 miles south. He had met them three days previously, and they were also awaiting the convoy.

With the vague air of a social director under whose auspices we had fallen, and as though he greeted and invited thousands of Canadian travelers to Adrar to cross with the convoy, Hermann assured us that he had a place we could stay and would soon intro- duce us to the others with whom we would be making the journey. Smilingly, we accepted his casual patronage, having nothing to lose by it.

Through some process that we didn't question, he had acquired squatter's rights to an empty house on the outskirts of town where we drove after leaving the hotel. Facing a large square, the old dwelling was rundown, deserted, and only accessible by a small gate in the high wall around the half acre of dusty yard in the rear. There was, however, a tap in the back which could be manipulated to produce a tired dribble of clear water, the most important item when we had everything else we needed. For a brief camping spot, it was quite satisfactory. Hermann himself was no longer staying at the house, choosing rather to keep close to his countrymen and future ride, a sentiment we well appreciated. After a brief inspection of the place, we gave him a ride to an open-air workshop on the far side of town to meet the other Germans.

NEW TRAVELING COMPANIONS

Geoff and I were, by this time, three weeks into Africa, brown from the sun, black stubble surrounding dry, cracked lips marking our weather-burned faces. Without hats, our hair fell uncontrollably in two or three directions, our clothes were well lived in, and we were a good deal leaner than we had been in Gibraltar days. I suppose we looked something like desert travelers, and the four Germans were our identical counterparts.

When we rolled up with Hermann, they were sitting around a small stove waiting for a pot of water to boil, and except for a seemingly disenchanted glance at our companion, continued watching the pot. I sensed immediately that we were not the first people Hermann had introduced to them, and that he was not as well-thought-of as he had led us to believe.

The shop was half-covered by a tin roof, the rest being open to the air, and the whole area surrounded by a high wall topped with broken glass. A Volkswagen minibus, obviously belonging to the Germans, was propped up on two bricks, and an Arab was working on one of the rear wheels. Camping gear lay on the ground on all sides, attesting to the fact that they had not just arrived for repairs that day.

Taking the initiative from Hermann, I said "good evening" in German, one of about three expressions I remembered from a year of studying that language in high school. One of the fellows, Hans, got up to acknowledge the greeting and shake hands, the others remaining seated disinterestedly around the blackened pot, which was just beginning to steam. From this dull meeting was born a most extraordinary friendship.

Hans was clearly the leader of the group. He looked like a young lion—fit, tanned, and blue-eyed. He was well muscled, though not tall, and he had an air of authority about him. He was the kind of person who could take in all the details of a situation quickly, make a decision, and then act.

Hermann stepped forward to explain what they were doing in Adrar and where they were going, which immediately put us on a common footing. Josef, the tallest of the group, invited us to join them for coffee. With a jumble of French, English, German and Spanish, plus Hermann translating occasionally, we soon became quite friendly, joking about the various incidents that had preceded our separate arrivals to join the same convoy in that little town.

They had left Munich the same day we had left Gibraltar and had experienced as many problems of various sorts as we, their most recent being a back wheel that had bogged down in the sand outside Adrar, with the spline sheared from the inside of the wheel drum. For three days they had been camped at the blacksmith-type garage, while the Arab mechanics fiddled with various ways of repairing it, none having been discovered. When we left one hour later, after a good deal of laughter, we assured them that we would come by in the morning to see how they were getting along. The seeds of chumdom were beginning to grow.

MISSING OBJECTS

Prudently moving everything stealable inside the gate, we set up camp that night in the yard under the stars, preferring the ground to the dirty cement floor inside the house. In the morning we cooked breakfast and then visited the little marketplace off the main square to see if there were any vegetables for sale, before returning to shave and wash our clothes. Foolishly, we had left our belongings in the yard, and much to our chagrin, our one camera and an alarm clock had vanished in our absence. Considering that we would likely never have another chance to take photographs of the desert ahead, the loss of the camera was a minor disaster.

Mad as hatters, we drove straight to the old police station and raised a fuss, committing the police chief to do everything in his power to recover the items. He climbed into his black official Citroen and followed us back to the house, the speedy arrival of the two vehicles scattering a band of ragged urchins playing near the gate. Harshly, he shouted at them to come back, which they did, terrified, skulking like whipped puppies. Two of the brats were trembling so much they could barely speak, but all denied any knowledge of the theft. The Arab police chief rubbed his swarthy mustache and shrugged, insisting that such a thing never happened in Adrar and promised further inquiries. We never saw the camera or the alarm clock again.

We learned an important lesson: *Never become too complacent or overconfident. In life, the most successful people are invariably those who are the most fastidious about the critical details of their work. They don't take things for granted or trust to chance. They know that it's the details that will get you every single time.*

Back at the shop, the repair job was proceeding at a snail's pace, causing the Germans to begin worrying about being ready in time to leave with the convoy. Hans, the leader of the group, came with us to check with the truck drivers camped on the edge of town. There was no need to be concerned, they assured us. They weren't leaving until the next day, or maybe the day after. We returned to the garage to urge the Arab mechanic to hurry. He merely gave us a bored shrug. There wasn't enough "get up and go" in that garage to fill a teacup.

We sat in the shade pondering some method to pass the time. After a couple of minutes, Hans visibly brightened. "Would you like to go swimming?" he asked. He had to be joking; we hadn't seen enough water all together since we arrived in Algeria to take a bath. But Hans insisted he knew of a place if we could go in our Land Rover.

With the seven of us jammed into the vehicle, Geoff followed the directions out of town, the mid-morning sun almost overhead and the dashboard thermometer reading 110 degrees. Only five kilometers out of Adrar, a slash of bright green slowly emerged through the dancing heat waves. Another two kilometers brought us to a large vegetable farm, surrounded by a hedge and above which turned a steel windmill. Still following Hans' eager directions, we circled the perimeter to the far side, stopping at a gap in the thorn bushes. Quickly doffing our clothes for bathing trunks, we followed the four Germans through the hedge and across the cultivated rows.

There amid the melon plants and citrus trees was a large reservoir, 50 yards square and five feet deep, the brilliant algae-green water shining like a huge emerald. With a yell and a whoop, we were all in the water, splashing and diving, cavorting like exuberant porpoises. For two hours we stayed and played in the cool water, bothered by none but an old Arab who shouted at us and stalked away, muttering.

ONE WITH THE GERMANS

On the way back to Adrar, everyone laughing in high spirits, we made a critical decision. We told the Germans not to be too concerned about their car; if the trucks left before it was repaired, we could form a convoy of two and make the crossing together. We left them at the workshop, where a young Arab was slowly filing away at their wheel drum, and went "home" to sleep through the heat.

We had arrived in Gibraltar on April 20, and it was now May 30. Except for an increase in heat as we moved further south, the weather never varied. The sun rose clean and fresh about 5:30 a.m., climbed to its maximum height and intensity by 1 p.m., cooled by 6 p.m., and set shortly after 8 p.m. There were never any clouds, no mist, very little dew, and always a scarlet-red sunset to finish the day. Occasionally there was wind, but by and large the weather was consistently beautiful and completely dependable.

The mornings were fine and cool, and early rising was a pleasure. The evenings were warm but not hot, and the air was very dry, causing perspiration to evaporate rapidly. The gentle evening breezes came like soft caresses through our hair and into our open shirts, making idle contemplation a pleasurable pastime.

We had arrived in Gibraltar a full five pounds heavier than we'd left London, from the exercise and all the eating we had done on the way. Since arriving in Tangiers, we'd both lost 10 pounds and felt none the worse for it. We weren't eating much, and according to the books, we weren't eating well, but we were physically sound. We were sleeping better, though lighter, waking quickly and completely at the slightest noise. Our senses of hearing and sight were sharper, our reflexes faster, and our mental grasp of situations, as well as our adaptability to them, was much quicker. Even our ability to see the humor in a difficult situation was improved, though we had never been overly beset with pessimism.

In short, we felt more genuinely alive, mentally and physically, than we could ever remember being. We felt as though our senses had been polished a little, leaving us with a confident glow. We felt ready for anything—sing a song, write a book, cross a desert, love a girl, anything. And it was a nice feeling to have.

When we are living in total harmony with what we believe, we feel most alive—our senses are heightened, and we feel ready for anything.

Both in Béchar and in Adrar, the vast quietude of the Sahara Desert seemed to work in a strange manner on us, during those days of patient waiting for the next segment of the journey. Instead of increasing the need and desire for human companionship, that great empty land had the opposite effect on us. The feeling of solitude and the joy of being quietly alone with our thoughts became very precious, more so than they had ever been in the city. Geoff and I derived a great deal of pleasure from hours spent reading or writing, or just staring at the flickering embers of the tiny campfire, with scarcely more than a word passing between us. Even when we sat around in the evenings with the Germans, it was very much the same. And yet, without words, the bond joining the six of us set, and hardened, and bound our lives together in the course of three short days.

READY OR NOT

The next morning was Wednesday, and the Arab at the garage was still avoiding any serious work on the Germans' wheel drum. "Why don't you tell him to get a move on?" I asked Hans. He answered that none of them spoke French except Hermann, and the Arabs just ignored Hermann's meek inquiries. The whole idea of poking around at such a small job for five days was nonsense, and now that we had agreed to cross with the Germans, the minibus was now partially our problem.

Picking up the wheel drum, I took it to the Arab in charge of the workshop. Politely, in slow French, I told him that if the Volksbus wasn't ready to leave that evening with the convoy, not only would we finish the job ourselves, but he wasn't going to be paid one dinar for the five days he had already wasted.

With indignation, he launched into a long story about how hard he'd been working on it, and how much work he had to do in the garage. He said that he didn't realize the convoy was leaving so soon, and he didn't think it mattered how long the job took because we were waiting for the convoy anyway.

Carefully avoiding being outright rude, I repeated that the car must be ready by that night at the latest. I thrust the wheel rim into his hand and gave him a big grin, then turned and went back to where the Germans were sitting and watching. They hadn't understood anything except the object of the exchange.

The Arab examined the wheel drum for a second, then shouted at two of his assistants, who came running. Waving the drum in their faces, he berated them for their laziness, and pointing vigorously at the crippled Volksbus, relayed the urgency of getting the job done by that evening. They all looked at me as some sort of a traitor.

Now that the Arabs were making progress with the wheel drum, we left the Germans to begin repacking their vehicle.

When I returned to the shop in the late afternoon, I was told that the repair had been simple, a matter of welding new spline onto the sheared drums, but it was the filing of those new splines so that they would fit on the axle that was taking so long to finish. The man in charge insisted, however, that the job was almost finished.

The Germans were all packed to leave, and we agreed to meet at our "house" the next morning to cross with the convoy.

THE ISSUE OF TRAVELING COMPANIONS

Choose your friends and associates carefully. Work only with people you respect and whom you can count on. Take your time in assessing new people. Until they are tested "under fire," it is hard to assess their real character.

Your choice of a "reference group" in life can boost your success more than any other factor. The people with whom you must identify have an influence on how you think, feel, talk, and behave.

Your choice of traveling companions in life can decide the success or failure of the entire journey.

SECTION 6:
ONE OIL BARREL AT A TIME

Whatever your goal, you can achieve it by taking one step at a time. This is one of the greatest of all success principles. "By the yard it's hard; but inch by inch, anything's a cinch!"

Do you want to be financially independent? It begins by saving your first dollar, and then one dollar at a time. Do you want to be thin, fit, and healthy? This simply requires eating a little less and exercising a little more each day.

If one of your goals is to be among the top people at what you do, you can achieve it by reading one page at a time. You can practice and develop one skill at a time. You can learn and grow one day at a time.

Take your biggest goal and break it down into daily, even hourly, activities. Then discipline yourself to take the next step, and then the next and the next and the next.

Remember, happiness is the progressive, step-by-step realization of a worthy goal or ideal. And whatever someone else has done, you can probably do as well.

CHAPTER 20

THE CONVOY

We had just finished packing our things carefully back into the Rover the next morning, Thursday, when Hans and Helmut came roaring up in their Volksbus, cheering jubilantly and blasting the horn. The joy was infectious, and we all laughed at the thought of being on the road again. Geoff and I leaped into the Rover and raced pell-mell, bumper to bumper, back into town with the Germans.

The convoy had left at dawn, but they planned to stop at Reggane, 80 miles south, for the night, so we weren't pressed for time. After stocking up fully with gasoline and water, we checked the oil and water in the vehicles, as well as the tires, declared ourselves road ready, and set out to catch the trucks. After four days in Adrar, we were glad to see the last of it.

The Algerian government stamps your passport in Adrar, 500 miles north of the border, and as far as they're concerned, you no longer exist. If something happens to you in the desert, you're on your own.

The Arab truck drivers on the run from Oran and Algiers are a lazy lot. They carry bales of cheap textiles, tin pots and pans, canned fish and tomato paste, and other cheap, high-profit goods to be sold in the bazaars of sub-Saharan Africa. They are in no hurry and often stop for days at a time to visit friends and family on the road down. When they do drive, it is only for two or three hours in the morning and perhaps the same in the evening. They rarely drive at night, the time we preferred to travel, and the 2,000-mile trip to Gao or the 2,500 miles to Niamey, in Niger, usually takes them four weeks. The financial benefits of making better time didn't weigh too heavily on them.

It was not surprising, then, when only two hours out of Adrar we came upon three of the trucks that had left that morning stopped next to the "piste" for the midday heat. Since it was just 11 a.m. and the sun was becoming fierce, we waved to the Germans that stopping was not a bad idea, turning off and parking next to one of the trucks to get as much shade as possible.

There was a slight draft of hot air coming through the open doors of the vehicle, and the heat was terrible. The difference between three weeks and 400 miles north, as regards to the midday sun in the open desert, was ponderous. The temperature was 125 degrees in the meager shade of the vehicle. Struggling for breath in the searing atmosphere, sweat pouring off us in sticky rivulets, we drank and drank and drank, consuming five gallons between us in that five-hour period. Sleeping was out of the question, and eating disregarded utterly. We didn't have enough energy even to talk much, each of us thinking miserably, "If it's like this here, what will it be like when we get into the middle of the desert?" However, for the sake of the vehicles, we disciplined ourselves to stay until 4 p.m., when it had "cooled" to 100 degrees. Then we left the lumbering trucks and continued to Reggane.

Reggane is the last town in Algeria, although the frontier was 500 miles farther south, and it looked like the last town in Algeria. There was one lonely petrol pump about 200 yards from a cluster of brown buildings, several of which were deserted, the sand already beginning to fill their doorways. At one time there had been a Foreign Legion post there, but now it stood away from the houses, windblown and uninhabited. It was just before sunset that Thursday when we arrived, and the funereal atmosphere of the lifeless, darkened doorways made us willing to drive right on through.

We stopped the two vehicles by the lone gas pump and waited for someone to come and unlock it. When five minutes passed with no one in sight, Hermann said he would seek information about the convoy.

Before leaving Adrar, we hadn't seen too much of Hermann. He hadn't accompanied us swimming, always being in town chatting with storekeepers, police, and anyone else he could find. He was about 35 years old, and not our type of friend at all, so his little side trips didn't cause too much concern. Besides, he was constantly returning with gems of information about the area and the desert.

Eventually, a young Arab came running with the key to the pump, and we topped off our tanks. After filling the water containers at a nearby well, we followed the dirt road around and to one side of the settlement, meeting Hermann coming back. He had found the main convoy and learned that they weren't leaving until the next day—or perhaps the day after. He suggested that we camp somewhere nearby until they were ready to go.

GOING IT ALONE

We decided to hold a council. We had all had enough of Arab procrastination. The Germans were just as anxious as Geoff and I to cross the desert. The breakdowns, the holdups, the retracing of steps, the expenditures, the heat, the Arab mentality—all of it had worn our patience thin.

We discussed options by the Rover's headlamps while Helmut and Kurt made a large pot of coffee. The only reason we had waited for the convoy was for added insurance against a breakdown in the desert. But two vehicles, we reasoned, were enough insurance to get us over the last lap, especially since the convoy would be coming behind us. There was a waterhole marked on our map 450 miles south; if something happened to one of the vehicles, we could drive in the other vehicle, either back to Reggane or to the waterhole, or just sit tight until the convoy came along. Hans was in complete accord with us, and the other Germans went along with what he said, without argument. The only dissenter was Hermann.

Hermann now put his opinion forward, in the manner of one dealing with people who are in complete ignorance of a field in which he specialized. Having spent so much time gathering bits of information, he had apparently lost sight of the fact that we had all crossed the same rugged country to arrive in Reggane, and were equally aware of what lay ahead. He delivered his opinion confidently, pointing out that if both vehicles broke down, we could die before the slow-moving convoy came up. He went on to say that the only way to cross the Sahara was with a large group, for mutual protection. It was better to go slower and be assured of success than to take the chance of going alone. He ended by saying that he knew of a very good place for us to camp while we waited, as if that ended the discussion.

As it happened, Hermann was correct. But because we didn't like him, we rejected his ideas and input, refusing to consider their possible validity. *We made the mistake of focusing more on "who" was right or wrong rather than "what" was right.*

The Germans, with the exception of Hans, seemed hesitant. Geoff just looked at Hermann as though he had said something very foolish indeed, and then walked away. I finally told Hans that Geoff and I were leaving that night, convoy or no convoy. They must make up their own minds.

Hans looked me in the eyes for a few seconds in silence, and then, his mind suddenly made up, he turned to Hermann and told him that we were all leaving in half an hour. He could come or stay as he chose. Then we all sat down and drank the coffee.

Hans was clearly the leader of the group. Not only did he accept complete responsibility for every detail, but he never shrank from making a decision and taking action. He was as solid as a rock.

HOW LEADERS LEAD

More than anything, leaders lead by example. They demonstrate the qualities of courage, vision, and foresight. Above all, they emerge to make decisions and take command.

Leaders accept a high level of responsibility for results. They take initiative and are action-oriented. They don't wait for things to happen; they make them happen.

Each person can be a leader by deciding to act like a leader whenever the situation calls for it.

And we have never been more in need of leaders—at every level of our society—than we are today.

CHAPTER 21

THE CROSSING

The coffee was finished when Hermann finally decided he would come with us, but he didn't pretend to be pleased at having his advice ignored. His know-all attitude was beginning to grate on Geoff and me, and we were glad he was riding in the other vehicle. At 8 p.m., with the Volksbus leading, we pulled out of Reggane and drove into the dark toward the Tenezrouft, the heart of the Sahara.

According to the map, the road ran almost due south across the desert and deep into Mali. The first place we could get water was a dot called Bordji-Perez at the 450-mile mark. The route was broken at two places between Reggane and Bordji-Perez; at Poste Weygand and at Bidon Cinque-Poste Maurice Courtier. Geoff had learned about these two places in Algiers.

When the French controlled the Sahara, there was a steady stream of traffic across the desert into the colonies below. The two way stations were built by the Foreign Legion to allow travelers to break their journeys, make repairs, and restock with petrol and water. All travelers had to register at Reggane and deposit the equivalent of $300 per vehicle before starting across. The time of departure was noted and radioed to the next post, a set time being allowed for the traveler to report before vehicles were dispatched from either end to find him. The $300 was to cover any expenses incurred by the French government on behalf of the traveler, and was returned in Gao upon arrival. There were several facts that necessitated these precautions.

Since the Sahara officially became French territory, late in the 19th century, over 2,000 people had perished there. Many more were never found and were presumed dead. The deadly heat is the fiercest on earth. A lightly dressed man who collapsed in the open sun at 1 p.m. would expire through dehydration within 20 minutes. A person without a hat could suffer sunstroke, irreparable brain damage, or even death after only one hour at midday. The safe water ration in the summer months was set at five gallons per person per day. Crossing the Sahara was rightfully made out to be a very serious business.

When the French withdrew from their colonies in Africa, the new government of Algeria abandoned the desert outposts and lifted all restrictions on travel. We had been officially stamped out of Algeria in Adrar, and we were on our own. We were crossing at our own risk, and there would be no inquiry if we never came out. Having full confidence in our vehicle, however, we were not frightened at the prospect, but like soldiers before a battle, we certainly had something to think about.

CLEAR GOAL, HARD GOING

Our goal for the first night was the second of the abandoned way stations, Poste Maurice Cortier, two thirds of the distance. If we could get there before the sun caught us the next day, we would have shelter and only 150 miles to go the next night, to the well at Bordji-Perez. The difficult part of the crossing would then be behind us.

From the first, the piste (road) was very bad: 50 years of heavy traffic and several years of neglect had left it a mess of ruts, holes, and bumps. In countless places, the drifting sand had covered the road with a layer of fine powder, often to a depth of 18 inches—and in stretches of as much as 200 feet. It was in one of these dry swamps that our troubles began.

We were perhaps 20 miles along. Geoff was driving, and the Land Rover was about one quarter mile in front of the minibus. The sensation of hitting the soft sand was that of all four tires dropping to half pressure simultaneously. Geoff shifted from fourth, to third, to second, to get more torque, and then into four-wheel drive. With the motor screaming and the front tires digging in, we slowly moved out of the patch onto the firmer road ahead.

"Guess we'd better wait and see if they get through," said Geoff, as he pulled to the side and shifted the transmission into neutral. We got out and watched the approaching headlamps from opposite sides of the vehicle. As the roaring Volksbus hit the silt, the sand rose in a spray like splashing water, the vehicle careening from side to side drunkenly. Still it kept coming, but slower and slower until it came at last to a tired halt. As it stopped, the dust billowed past it, across the headlamps, in thick rolls. Hans was already out and inspecting the sunken back end.

Without a word, Geoff got into the Rover and started backing it up. I walked over to the vehicle and asked Hermann if they had a tow rope. They did, and while Helmut dug for it, everyone gathered around and looked at the wheels. They were buried to the frame in the sand and barely visible.

Even with the Rover pulling, the Volksbus refused to budge. We put our backs into it and tried again. It moved a little and then once more bogged down. We would have to dig it out and try it with the wheels clear.

While Geoff maneuvered the Rover forward and back to pull from an angle on undisturbed sand, Hans and I started digging underneath the rear wheels with machetes, Josef and Helmut working on the other side and Kurt helping Geoff with the rope. There was nothing casual about our attitude toward the job. We scrambled frantically to get the bus out and get going again. We dreaded being caught by the sun without protection, and we had a long way to go to reach that protection. Yet as fast as we dug, the sand ran back in, and soon we were all dripping with perspiration, including Geoff and Kurt, who had started digging with pots at the front tires.

HAPLESS HERMANN

The last one to descend from the bus had been Hermann, and while we were working, he stood back and watched us like an interested spectator. After a couple of minutes, he came over and said we must get all the sand out from around the wheels, as if we weren't already trying to do just that. We had better not drive any-more in the dark, he added, then climbed back into the vehicle and laid down. We were concentrating too hard on the digging to pay attention to him.

In another five minutes, we had the wheels as clear as we were going to get them, and with the Land Rover pulling, the wheels of the Volksbus spinning, and the four of us straining every sinew, it slowly began to move—10 feet, 20 feet, 40 feet, and then it stopped. We stopped too, lungs and legs burning from the exertion. Geoff had just come back to see how it was going when Hermann stuck his head out the window to inspect the proceedings. That was too much, even if he was a minister. Puffing and wiping the salty sweat from my nose, I walked around the bus and yanked the side door open.

"Get out!" I panted. "You can damn well get out and work with the rest of us."

"I thought the work was all finished," he replied in an offend-ed tone as he climbed out onto the sand.

"Well, the work is not all finished," I said, and pointing to the rear of the bus, added, "You can push from there, until the bloody thing is out."

"You take a turn at driving," Geoff said quietly. "I'll kick him in the ass if he looks like he's slacking off."

Hermann petulantly took up a pushing position against the back of the Volksbus, and Hans changed with Helmut as driver. When I got back into the Rover, I gave a blast on the horn and let out the clutch full throttle, slowly inching forward until the Rover was on solid roadbed. We were out.

On small teams, everyone has to do his or her fair share. Everyone has to pitch in to get the job done. Everyone is responsible for the end result. No one can stand aside and expect someone else to do more while he or she does less.

As Hans untied the rope, we all cheered and laughed, climbing happily back into our respective vehicles. Even Hermann looked pleased, though guiltily, his face dripping from the effort. We pushed on relieved, eager to make up the lost time, a bit delighted at having met an obstacle and surmounted it as a team, but hoping that the necessity would not arise again. Our relief was short-lived. Ten minutes later the Rover piled into another drift. We just managed to get clear when the Volksbus came in behind us and bogged down again. This time Hans didn't spin the back wheels—the frantic effort that only dug the minibus in deeper. We leaped out of the vehicles before the dust had settled and muscled the van out with brute strength. Not stopping to rest in our urgency, we yelled and cheered each other on, chanting and straining on every third count until it came clear. This time we were too out of breath to rejoice. We just climbed back in and drove on.

For the next five hours, the pattern of bogging down and muscling out repeated itself, over and over again, until we were ready to collapse from exhaustion. Sometimes we could use the Land Rover to pull or push, but most of the time we had to push it out by hand, lungs screaming and every muscle straining painfully.

But no one was complaining, and after the incident with Hermann, no one shirked. Everyone gave the best they had to give, every time they had to give it, no matter how tired they were. It never occurred to Geoff and me that we were breaking our backs for a vehicle that wasn't ours, owned by fellows we'd never met until a few days ago, and whom we'd probably never see again after the crossing.

A SILENT PACT

We had formed an unbreakable pact, not in words but by implication. From the first, when we said we'd wait for them if the convoy left before their vehicle was repaired, the fabric binding our seven lives together began to interweave and entangle. We were caught up in it and carried forward, inextricably, powerfully, feeling the strength of the bond growing over the miles. There in the desert, we were the only people on earth. Every bit of our separate lives, every laugh, every tear, every success and every failure, had played its part bringing us together at that time and place in the middle of that wasteland.

We were chained by fate into one small struggling mass of humanity pitted against the desert. When we heaved together in the powder-fine sands to extricate a Volksbus, it was not *their* Volksbus, it was *the* Volksbus, and it was pulled out by *the* Land Rover. We succeeded or failed together, as one indivisible entity. And the strength of the bond lay in the strength of the individuals who formed that bond. No one could give any less than his best, for our entire beings, and to a lesser extent, our very lives, depended on defeating 450 miles of unfeeling sand.

There was little conversation, as discussion was irrelevant. In a way not understood by us, we were caught up in something that transcended words and philosophy, something very strong, and something that couldn't be clearly examined until the journey was finished. And it couldn't be finished unless and until we reached the water at Bordji-Perez.

What often kills a marriage or merger or partnership is the notion of his or hers, mine and yours, ours and theirs. When you're in the Sahara—or in any significant challenge—such distinctions will spell death. You must believe "We're all in this together."

FROM ROUGH TO SMOOTH

By 2 a.m., we had been clear of heavy sand for almost an hour, but the going was still very rough on the vehicles, and on us, so we signaled a stop and suggested a 20-minute coffee break. The fatigue from the long day before and the five hours of steady exertion that had marked most of the time since leaving Reggane was making itself felt on all of us.

While the water boiled on the Germans' stove, the vehicles positioned in such a way that the headlights of each fell on the other, we hauled out our petrol containers and refilled the tanks. The miles of strain and high revs in getting in and out of the sand had taken a toll on the precious amber fluid. Also, something was wrong with the carburetor on the Volksbus, causing it to use too many liters of petrol for too few kilometers. Hans and Geoff took the carburetor apart and cleaned it over coffee, then reassembled it carefully. On we went.

The track was still shaking the Rover violently, and without a moon, the endless country beyond the range of the lights appeared dark and forbidding. But a thought occurred to me. The reason we were staying on the rough piste was that, if we strayed off it and couldn't find it again, we would be lost in the desert. But, I thought, since the road runs straight north and south, if we deliberately drove off it to the west, it would always have to be to the east. The open country was probably a lot smoother than the worn track, and we couldn't possibly get lost as long as we kept the road on one side.

Swinging the Rover up over the sandy ridge bordering the track, I drove an eighth of a mile straight west, telling Geoff what I had in mind at the same time. Leveling off and running parallel to the piste, it was obvious we'd made a very useful discovery. The open country stretched flat and unbroken to the furthermost reaches of the headlamps. The bouncing and rattling that had kept us peering ahead for deep ruts was gone. We were free to swing to the right or the left, or drive in circles if we wanted. From a narrow broken track 10 yards wide, we had come upon a sand-gravel highway the length and breadth of the Sahara between the piste and the Atlantic Ocean, 1,800 miles to the west.

I swerved back over to the piste to stop and let the Germans catch up with us, explaining the idea to Hermann. But he balked. It was too risky, he said. The piste was the only safe place to travel if we didn't want to get lost in the night, and besides, we shouldn't be driving at night anyway. I asked him if he could explain the idea to Hans and Helmut, the drivers, and let them decide, which he did, in a discouraging tone of voice. Leaving them to work it out for themselves, we drove along parallel with them for a few minutes, varying the distance from a hundred yards to a quarter mile.

Hermann had obviously made a fuss about it to get back at us for having made him sweat a little, because the Volksbus stayed on the uneven piste for several more kilometers. Then, all at once it swerved and lurched over the sand ridge, off the piste, and came straight for us. Just before reaching us it leveled off and we drove side by side, laughing and honking at the newfound sensation of freedom. I don't know what was said between the fellows and Hermann in that brief interim, but after that incident, he didn't have so many suggestions to make—and no one paid much attention to him when he did make them.

We stayed off the piste for the remainder of the night, always keeping it fairly close on the left. We had a wonderful feeling of freedom driving that way, sometimes close enough to touch the other vehicle, sometime swerving far out and cutting in on each other—turning just in time to avoid a collision. Most of the time, though, we drove about 100 yards apart, one or the other a little ahead, boring our way through the night with the stabbing headlights.

I learned an important lesson: *It is normal and natural for us to get into a comfort zone, a rut, and then resist every suggestion to get out of it—even if we're not happy with the results we're getting. We must continually be asking, "Could there be a better way?" We must deliberately force ourselves to try something new or different if the old way is no longer working.*

ABSOLUTE NOTHINGNESS

Even with the windows opened to let in the cool air, we were having real difficulties staying awake in the early hours of the morning. The first edge of light in the east somehow lifted the dull fatigue a little, and soon we could see the terrain. At the first clear view of it, I snapped wide awake and nudged Geoff, dozing on the seat beside me.

"Look at that, Geoff! Just open your eyes and take a good look!" Geoff shook his head numbly and leaned close to the windshield. Slowly his eyes widened and his jaw went momentarily slack. Then he sat back in his seat and just stared, silently. We had come to the end of the earth. We had arrived in a land where the nothingness was absolute. The barren terrain had begun in Morocco. As we had driven south, the land had weakened; the pulse had faded and diminished. The silent rattle of its last breath had touched us in the dark. Now, at last, the land was dead.

The Volksbus had fallen behind in the pre-dawn hours, and we were alone, pressed between the sky and the yellow sands, a lifeless void, with only the sound of the engine to break the eternal stillness.

Before us lay a flat, unbroken, yellow expanse that flowed away on all sides endlessly. Before there had been tufts of scraggly grass and a bit of rugged sagebrush refusing to heed the death knell; now there was only lifeless sand. Before, there had been a slight roll to the arid terrain that broke the monotony of the desert; now it was perfectly flat. Before, there had been a glimmer of hope that nature had not turned her back on the Sahara; now there was nothing.

The brilliant blue of the desert sky joined the dirty yellow of the desert floor in a perfect circle, of which we were the precise center, and remained so as we moved. The flaming gold of the sun, climbing high in the sky, was the one thing nature had bestowed on the last of the lands. *We felt as if we had come in on the middle of a colossal joke, being told by the sun to the unhearing sands, and its punchline was death.*

We slowed to let the Volksbus catch up with us, resolving not to lose sight of it again. When it came up about 10 minutes later, we increased our speed and stayed even with it. There were no more cheery grins and waves; the long, trouble-filled night had set us back too far on our proposed schedule. With the sun sitting on the horizon, like an evil yellow cat waiting to pounce on two silly mice a long way from their holes, the only thing that mattered now was mileage.

CROSSING YOUR SAHARA

The keys to great success have always been *focus* and *concentration. There are critical times in life when you must throw your whole heart—mind and body—into what you're doing in order to succeed.* Whenever you find something getting done, you find a monomaniac with a mission.

Once you begin, devote your entire time and attention to the task or goal. Never let up. Keep pushing until the objective is reached. Resolve to continue until the goal is 100 percent complete. This is the ultimate test.

CHAPTER 22

ONE OIL BARREL AT A TIME

Y ou couldn't get lost driving in the Sahara in the daytime. The piste is marked at five-kilometer intervals, exactly the curve of the earth, with black 55-gallon oil drums. At any given time, you can always see two oil drums, the one behind and the one ahead.

As you reach one oil drum, the next one, five kilometers ahead, pops up on the horizon, and the one five kilometers behind falls off, as if it had been shot in a shooting gallery.

All you have to do to cross the biggest desert in the world is to take it "one oil barrel at a time." I learned later in life that, *if you go as far as you can see to go at the moment, you'll see enough to go one step further. You can accomplish even the greatest goals "one oil barrel at a time."*

At 6:30 a.m., a small blot appeared on the horizon ahead. Some time later, we came to Poste Weygand, the 160-mile mark, after 11 hours of solid going. It consisted of three Quonset huts and a larger frame building, possibly an old barracks. Ghostlike and deserted, doors half ajar and windows broken, the buildings sat like tombstones, alone and abandoned. We didn't stop, and only slowed to read the blackened sign 100 yards past. White writing on a charred background, under a skull and crossbones, stated in French, "Do not leave the piste beyond this point." Ten minutes later we passed another blackened sign that stated simply, "Tropic of Cancer."

Now the sun really became the enemy. It first appeared in the east as a golden sliver of light along the horizon. Then the first roundness peeked over the horizon, as though looking for a victim. Slowly the entire sun rose into the sky and then sat silently on the horizon before beginning its inexorable climb toward midday.

Geoff and I entertained each other by quoting verses from "Carry On:"

> And so in the strife of the battle of life
> It's easy to fight when you're winning;
> It's easy to slave, and starve and be brave,
> When the dawn of success is beginning.
> But the man who can meet despair and defeat

With a cheer, there's a man of God's choosing;
The man who can fight to Heaven's own height
Is the man who can fight when he's losing.

Carry on, carry on. Things never were looming so black;
But show that you haven't a cowardly streak,
And though you're unlucky, you never are weak.
Carry on! Brace up for another attack.
It's looking like hell, but you never can tell.
Carry on, old man! Carry on!

The race for Bodin Cinque, the second abandoned army post, was on in earnest, although it was already lost. We knew it was impossible to cover 170 miles before the sun reached its fiery zenith. We had lost too much time in the struggles of the previous night. It was now a matter of how close we could get to that landmark.

The Land Rover was running beautifully. Throughout the strenuous night, it had never coughed, sputtered, or failed to respond to the continuous demands of pushing, pulling, and dragging through the clinging sands. The hum of the 96-horse-power engine transmitted its confidence through our weariness, letting us feel that, whatever might lie ahead in the way of difficulties, our vehicle would remain one constant dependable factor.

The Volksbus, however, was having troubles. The battered machine gave the impression that it was going along with this mad idea, but it in no way approved. From the first time it was driven off the paved roads, it began to protest. If it was driven over a hard bump, a tire would blow out. If driven in heavy sand, it would bog down and refuse to budge. Now that it had been betrayed into coming so far into the desert, it refused to run properly, gobbling petrol greedily. Several times in the night we had stopped and adjusted the carburetor in vain efforts to cut down on its gluttonish consumption. And as the heat increased that morning, the Volksbus ran even worse, forcing us to go slower.

HOT, HOTTER, HOTTEST

The ideal cruising speed of the Rover was 35 miles an hour. With the firm unbroken terrain, we should have been driving at maximum speed the whole time, but we were lucky to do 25 mph without leaving the Volksbus behind. Meanwhile, the sun continued its relentless climb, burning away the early morning chill by the time Poste Weygand had fallen off the horizon behind us.

We began to pass the remains of vehicles that had not survived the crossing. Usually they were just shapeless masses of colorless scrap—all usable parts having been stripped by other travelers. On three occasions, though, the automobiles were in good condition, complete with tires, seats, and windows. They were locked tightly, as though their owners had parked them minutes before and then vanished. Just after 10:30, we came to one of these, a Renault-Dauphine, sitting a few yards off the barely discernible piste.

Stopping to scavenge anything of possible use, we soon saw there was nothing of value left in it or on it, except the tires, and we were too exhausted to consider taking them off. Climbing back into our vehicles to escape the blistering rays of the overhead sun, we urgently hurried on. But minutes later, the Volksbus developed a vapor lock and came to a halt. The fuel pump on the Rover was also acting up with the heat, and the engine quit as we approached the vehicles. We had no choice. We were there for the day.

At 11 a.m., the thermometer read 110 degrees, and the air was already stiflingly hot. Geoff dragged a full jerry-can of water out of the back and onto the seat between us. Now that the vehicle was no longer moving, the relief from the heat afforded by the air currents had ceased. Breathing became laborious, and conversation an effort best avoided. Trickles of sweat began to flow down our faces to mingle with the soaked stench of our shapeless T-shirts and drip onto the seats where we sprawled, drained of strength after 30 hard hours without sleep. Outside, the noiseless inferno of golden rage pounded down in merciless fury on the two little vehicles that represented the only life in the very heart of hell.

The mercury began to climb inexorably inside the glass tube of the thermometer. By noon the temperature was 120 degrees and rising, as though to mock the inert figures in the soundless vehicles, where the only motion was the slow tilting of water bottles to quench a thirst that parched the throat and swelled the tongue, thick and rubbery. The only noise in the scorching stillness was the steady gasping that never quite filled the straining lungs. We were all exhausted, and semi-conscious, but sleep was impossible. Motion was unthinkable. Just to breathe and to drink took every bit of strength we had. And still the temperature climbed.

At 1:20 p.m. the red line had stopped rising at 130 degrees of searing, broiling, terrible heat. The yellow sands had turned a dazzling, blinding white, flinging the glare at us from all directions. The only relief was in the blank, listless staring at the brown canvas top, heads lolled back like those of rag dolls. The minutes never passed and the hours lasted forever. The thirst was unquenchable; a quart of water disappeared in three spasmodic swallows, a single gurgling slurp, and minutes later the throat was so dry it took a choking effort to swallow. The intensity of the bake-oven temperature was unbelievable, unbearable, and inescapable. It was an incredible feeling to be held in one spot, immovable and suffering, in the middle of nothing, with only the sun above and the sand disappearing into the distance on all sides.

By 2 p.m., the mercury had begun its slow descent, and by 4:30 it had sunk below 110 degrees for the first time in almost seven hours. We were utterly debilitated, feeling only a vague wonderment that the ordeal was finally over. Our 40 liters of water had dwindled to 10, and the Germans' supply wasn't much better. Everyone looked haggard, and a bit stunned, after the ferocity of the day, as we numbly adjusted ourselves in our seats and started on. We were just halfway to Bodji-Perez and if we didn't get there before the heat of the next day, we would be in serious trouble.

REVIVAL AND REPAIRS

The semiconscious state we were in before we were stopped by heat and exhaustion had changed very little, but with the motion of the vehicle and the decline in temperature of the dwindling day, the run-over feeling gradually gave way to a tired patience. Spirits had also risen among our comrades. When the Volksbus pulled level with us, Josef and Hans were sitting on the roof wearing old pith helmets and looking for all the world like two hardy explorers who'd lost their camels.

Hans had a pair of binoculars and was scanning the horizon when he took them from his eyes and pointed to a dot far ahead, indicating that we should stop there. The dot slowly took form and became a Taurus van, very similar to the Volksbus, sitting perfectly intact a quarter mile off the piste.

We coasted to a stop next to it. The Germans were out and all over it before the engines had died, forcing open the locked doors and the hood to get at the seats and the motor.

With a dexterity that amazed and delighted Geoff and me, every spare part and accessory was detached and stored away in the Volksbus—the radiator, the fuel pump, the carburetor, the distributor, all the spark plugs, and most of the loose wiring. The two front tires found their way off the vehicle and onto the roof rack, leaving in a very short time a half-wrecked hull.

Since we had eaten nothing that day and were stopped anyway, we agreed to rejuvenate our flagging constitutions with a little nourishment. Besides, there was work to be done on the Volksbus if it was going to reach Bordji-Perez. The sun was low in the west by this time, and the terrible heat was gone for another day. But a soft breeze came up, making it difficult to operate the stove. The Sahara was not about to forgive us easily for coming so far. The inside of the van provided some shelter, and the beans and sausage were soon steaming in the pan.

We were eating more from necessity than hunger—the sun and the fatigue having destroyed our appetites. We found that the food tasted like chalk in our still-swollen mouths. We gave up the idea of eating after a few laborious mouthfuls, but we could still drink. Geoff soon had a pot of tea brewed, into which he sliced one of our three lemons and added half a cup of sugar.

That was the most delicious drink I had ever tasted in my life. I had partaken of lemon tea many times over the years, as had Geoff, but until we drank that steaming, sweet, tangy liquid in the middle of the Sahara, it seemed that we had never been thirsty before, and never quenched a thirst in so regal a manner. We made pot after pot, gulping it down, letting its warmth flow and sing through our tired limbs, erasing the hardships of the day and the apprehension of the night. There was nothing special about the ingredients, nor anything unusual about the taste as lemon tea goes, but in that place and at that time, it was nectar such as the gods on Olympus had never tasted.

When we were at last satiated and the dishes stored back in the Rover, we joined the Germans at the rear of their vehicle to see how the repairs were coming along. They had adjusted the carburetor and changed the points and were trying to start the engine. But for some reason, it refused to fire. Geoff started the Rover, and we gave the minibus a push in a circle that brought it back to where we had started. It still showed no sign of life. After changing the points again, we pushed the bus in a larger circle, at a faster speed, but got no response from the engine at all.

Now it was serious. A car that wouldn't start in these conditions, with our water supply almost depleted and the next well almost 200 miles away, must be repaired quickly or abandoned, and we all knew it. By the powerful beams of the Rover's headlamps, Hans, Geoff and I worked impatiently to find the fault—the other three fellows standing by, unable to help, while Hermann lay prostrate on the sand nearby, snoring.

Nothing we tried made any difference; there was no spark in the electrical system to fire the plugs. As our irritation at the unsolvable riddle grew by the minute, our tired hands and weary minds refused to function properly, causing us to drop the tools and confuse each other with unworkable solutions. We started to snap at each other from frayed nerves and frustration. We were reaching the end of our rope, and still nothing was being accomplished. I dropped the screwdriver I'd been working with, walked back to the Rover, reached in, and switched off the lights.

Angrily, Geoff stood up and glared at me. "What the hell do you think you're going? How do you expect us to see?"

"Enough is enough," I said tiredly. "We're calling a halt. We're just too washed out to think clearly, let alone find out what ails the bloody thing. I vote we all lay down for an hour and then try it again."

Hans was standing by Geoff, eyes blazing at the interruption in the light. When I explained to him what I told Geoff, he wearily nodded in agreement. "You're right about us being wiped out," sighed Geoff. "We're getting nowhere this way."

Like seven corpses, we all stretched full length on the sand around the silent vehicles and dozed into half-sleep. No one slumbered; our nerves were too taut for that, but by 10 p.m. our heads were a little clearer and we went back to the motor while Helmut and Kurt boiled water for coffee. Hermann hadn't moved.

We agreed, as we worked, that if the minibus wasn't started by midnight, we would have to leave it. With what water we had left, we couldn't possibly survive another day in the sun.

Then it dawned on Hans what was wrong. Silently, he unscrewed the two bolts anchoring the distributor, removed it, and held it in the light. Dismantling it to expose the condenser, and then unscrewing it also, he peered at the tiny wire inside and broke into a triumphant grin. The wire had worn through without breaking, making it impossible to see until it was removed and examined under light at a certain angle. Excited with relief, we quickly replaced the condenser with a new one from the well-equipped spares kit on the roof rack. Reassembled and fastened tight, the engine caught with an angry snort and ran perfectly. It was 11:50 p.m.

After gulping down the coffee, we were on our way immediately. Barring any unforeseen incident, we had enough time to make Bordji-Perez.

ON AGAIN, OFF AGAIN

We passed through Bidon Cinque two and a half hours later, both vehicles running smoothly—the Volksbus running at a good speed for the first time and keeping up with, and ahead of, the Rover the whole way. The second way station was much larger than Poste Weygand, and was in much worse condition. Wells were caved in, the windows were broken, and all the wooden buildings had been gutted by fire. The desert was well on its way toward reclaiming it and blotting it out, sand having filled the Quonset huts to a depth of three feet. There was a haunted, lifeless shroud of stillness hanging over the post and after a quick inspection, we were glad to get away from it.

At 2:30 that morning, we figured that we had eight hours to travel the 80 miles to Bordji-Perez. It seemed that the difficulties were all behind us. We were on the downhill side of the run at last. Then we made the mistake that nature never lets pass: *we became overconfident, and then complacent, about our inevitable success, speeding up to hurry the process along. And that was when the problems began.*

Just 30 minutes outside Bidon Cinque, the Volksbus came to a sand-spraying, lurching halt with the left rear wheel off and the axle buried deep in the ground. I swung the Rover around and came up with the lights so we could view it clearly. It was worse than bad. The wheel had shaken loose, shearing its nut and cotter pin, and instead of falling off and rolling clear, it had jammed under the fender as the vehicle dug into the sand. Before it could even be examined properly, it had to be dug out, jacked up, and braced. The splash of dust hadn't yet settled when Hans was out and digging with both hands.

There was little room to work, and it was slow, painstaking labor. About 40 minutes passed in digging, jacking, bracing, re-jacking, re-bracing, and prying before the wheel came out and the truth was known. The only question was, "Can we fix it, or do we leave it?" As tight as we were with the Germans, the answer was as important to us as it was to them.

We determined that the wheel could be fixed, temporarily anyway. The spline on the axle had not sheared, only that on the wheel nut and the drum. We hammered the wheel back on and held it fast with another nut, finishing the job by jamming a thin screwdriver through the axle in place of a cotter pin.

It was 4 a.m. when our "convoy" moved out again. We knew the wheel wouldn't hold for very long, but then, it didn't need to. Hans was taking no chances. He drove as though he had a cargo of eggs on board. We followed slowly behind to watch for any sign of wobble in the crippled wheel.

For the next hour, all went well. Hans avoided any swerving or increases of speed that might antagonize the shaky wheel. With only 45 miles separating us from water and the dawn just beginning to glow in the eastern horizon, it looked as though we would make it after all. Again we became confident, and again the wheel wobbled, came loose, jammed under the fender, and ground the Volksbus to a sickly halt.

The work began anew in silence. It was exactly the same as the first time—the same order of jacking and bracing, the same division of labor, the same slow, sweating process. Hermann was asleep on the sand as the sun came up, and the wheel came off once more.

The drum was worse this time, and our choices of procedure were limited to one—the same as before. As long as there was the slightest chance we could get the Volksbus to Bordji-Perez, we entertained no thought of leaving it. Hans hammered the wheel back on, forced the half-stripped nut onto the axle, and banged a new screwdriver into the hole to hold it a little longer.

The sun sat on the eastern horizon to mock our efforts for a few minutes, then began to move ominously up the sky. We kept track of its relentless progress—grimly, through sunken eyes—as we carefully nursed the tired Volksbus. The fiery orb had watched and waited; now it was coming in for the kill.

With 30 miles to go, the wheel fell off again. It was the same story—same digging, jacking, repair job, new screwdriver for the axle, wake Hermann and carry on.

At 9:30 a.m., the wheel fell off again, deeper this time, taking 45 minutes to dig it out and hammer it back on. Still, we were not worried, as it was only 19 miles to Bordji-Perez.

But now the desert was beginning to bake. For the fourth time, the beaten shaky wheel sheared and fell off. Hans dragged the worn jack to the wheel and mutely began to dig. Tapping him on the shoulder gently, I pointed to the sun ablaze in the sky and shook my head; it was no use. We were out of screwdrivers, out of water, out of patience, and out of time.

Geoff was already undoing the back of the Land Rover and together, we unloaded everything onto the ground except the two sleeping bags. The Germans climbed inside, bringing some food and two empty water containers. We left everything else where it lay, and hoping the map was right about the water, we drove on down the road.

DEALING WITH ADVERSITY

Adversity brings out the best in you. It shows you what you are really made of, and makes you even better. When you embark on any new venture, you will have an unending series of obstacles and difficulties you could never have foreseen. But this is the "testing time" where you show your true character—and everyone is watching.

CHAPTER 23

BORDJI-PEREZ

We had been driving for 20 minutes, slowly so as not to overheat the vehicle, when the antennas atop the military post of Bordji-Perez appeared above a small rise, far off to the left. Leaving the piste, we drove straight over the rise toward the first sign of life we'd seen in what felt like two months. It consisted of a group of featureless mud buildings, completely encircled by a loose array of barbed wire. In front of the buildings was a large open area, also enclosed in the same barbed wire but having two wide gaps, obviously for access to the post from the road. Against a small clump of dark green bushes, on the side of the open space near the buildings, we could make out one lone water pipe with a tap on the end.

It was 11:15, and the blistering heat was rising. In the packed Land Rover, we were already sweating profusely. With our water now gone, the only thing on our minds was the quenching of the growing thirst that had already dried our mouths and parched our throats. Without slowing, I drove the vehicle through the first gap in the wire and stopped at the tap.

We had made it. Haggard, dirty, exhausted, and thirsty, we had nonetheless reached water. We had beaten the desert, after a hard battle, and the spoils were ours. Silently, we piled out of the Rover and converged on the tap.

THE POLITICS OF WATER

Geoff was just about to turn on the water when he was suddenly stopped by an angry, incomprehensible shout. Led by an unshaven Arab in a dirty undershirt, six ragged Algerian soldiers hurried from the nearest building, rifles pointed at us as they waved us away from the tap.

"What are you doing here?" demanded the undershirted Arab in French as he came up and stood between us and the water pipe. The rag-tag mob following him got into line and brandished their ancient weapons foolishly.

"We need a little water," I told him.

"Where have you come from?" he demanded, folding his arms across his flabby chest. "Why are you here? Why have you driven up to my fort? Where are your papers?"

He turned to the soldiers to see that they were taking it all in and had their weapons fixed on us. Then he turned back arrogantly and sneered, waiting for answers.

We were taken completely off-guard by the barrage of questions and had no idea why he was carrying on in such a manner. We were tired and dirty, not in the least bit offensive, and obviously unarmed. We didn't even know there was a military post at Bordji-Perez. I tried to explain our position.

"We came from Reggane. We've been in the desert for two days, and one of our vehicles is broken; we had to leave it. We need water and shelter from the sun, that's all."

"Where are your papers? Where is the other vehicle? I demand to see the other vehicle! Why have you entered the fort without permission? Give me your papers immediately!" He kept looking back at the others for approval.

Geoff got our passports from under the seat and gave them to him, but with the exception of Hermann, the Germans had left theirs in the Volksbus. The Arab glared at the passports and demanded in a louder voice, "Where are the other passports? I want to see the others!"

"The others are in the broken vehicle about 10 kilometers from here," I tried to explain. "We need water and protection from the sun until evening. We can bring the other passports to you then."

The sun was pounding down on our bare heads from directly overhead, and we were getting thirstier by the minute, our mouths too dry to lick our cracked lips. And this idiot seemed to think he was some sort of god.

"Who is German?" he demanded, waving Hermann's passport. "I know German from the war. I speak good German. Who is German?"

Hermann stepped forward and spoke to him in German, trying to explain again what happened and that we needed water. It was obvious the Arab could barely understand the German he was supposed to speak so well, but when Hermann switched into French, he irately silenced him and demanded that he continue in German, looking over his shoulder cockily at his men. Finally, he seemed to get the picture, nodding with a know-it-all smirk, as though it were a pack of lies.

The gate we had entered to approach the water pipe lay at one end of the rectangular-shaped yard, about 200 yards away. Opposite the front of the "fort" where we were standing, about 20 yards away, was another gap in the wire, seemingly the main gate from the worn look about the ground. The Arab pointed to the nearby gap in the wire and said, "That is the water gate. You must come through that gate for water." We had entered through the wrong gate, and he would not give us any water until we came through the correct one.

"Oh, for hell's sake, let's go through the right stinking gate and get something to drink," snapped Geoff. "I'm dying of bloody thirst."

We were all tense with anger when we got back in the Land Rover. Helmut and Josef started to walk to the gate, rather than ride the short distance, but they were stopped at gunpoint. They must also go in the vehicle, they were told. Everyone must do the same thing.

I started driving toward the water gate, seething with anger at the unbelievable stupidity of the whole situation. But the pompous little Arab started shouting and waving again. I quickly halted the Rover.

"You cannot drive straight to the water gate," he stated indignantly. "You must go back the same way you came in and drive to the outside of the water gate."

It was utterly ridiculous. We were 10 yards from the gate at that moment and the other gate was 200 yards back. Speechless, teeth gritted to keep from swearing at him, I swung the Rover around and headed back the way we had come, out the gate, along the perimeter of the wire, across the front of the fort, and back to the water gate—almost a quarter of a mile to go 10 yards. And the farce was not yet over.

The loud-mouthed little Arab had put on a dirty shirt and was waiting for us with eight men. Shouting again, he ordered us out of the vehicle and away from it. It had to be searched before we could have any water.

If they had rehearsed it, they couldn't have looked stupider. The vehicle—with the exception of the sleeping bags, the food, and the water containers—was quite empty. Yet each soldier fell out of line and took a turn coming over and poking his rifle in, then his head, to look around. Meanwhile, the Arab declared that he was keeping our passports until he had not only the other passports but also the broken-down vehicle for inspection, to verify that we had not sold it to someone in the desert.

"Fine, fine," we agreed. "Now can we have a little water, and for the love of God, some shade from the sun?"

But, oh no. We couldn't come near the fort to sit in the shade. There was a stone hut about a quarter of a mile away where we must go to get out of the sun. As for water, we would have to come two at a time to the front gate and ask the guard on duty for permission to fill the containers. With that, he strutted into the fort like a bantam rooster, clutching our passports in his dirty hand.

At that moment, if we'd had weapons or any chance of success with our bare hands, we would have stormed that post and murdered every man in the place. We were all pent up with a hate that was only a few degrees short of uncontrollable. I'd never felt that way in my life, nor had I ever thought myself capable of such an emotion. Our eyes were narrowed to slits and our jaws set rigidly to contain the burning rage within us as we drove to the hut. Even Hermann was gripped with the intensity of the sudden lust to kill.

Abigail Adams once wrote, "All men would be tyrants if they could." I've learned in life that people, given a little authority, will often abuse their power for no other reason than to prove to others that they have it. These people can be dangerous.

A LITTLE WATER, AT LAST

The hut was occupied by two Taureg holy men who were engaged in prayer when we walked in. There was a large earthen pot of cool water in one corner, and without so much as a by-your-leave, we passed it around until it was empty. The praying continued, and so we brought in the things from the Rover and laid out the sleeping bags on the dirt floor. Somewhat cooled, temperamentally and physically, and paying no more attention to the Tauregs than if they had been fenceposts, we sprawled out on the open bags and dozed off.

We couldn't sleep long, and we didn't sleep well. The tin-roofed hut was cooler than outside, but it soon turned into a sweatbox, and flies descended on us in swarms. After a couple of hours, it was too uncomfortable to sleep, and we were too tired to care, so with a few scraps of wood, plus the loan of a blackened pot from our co-inhabitants, we cooked up a stew of noodles and gravy that was devoured to the last morsel.

Hermann and Kurt were the first to make the trek for water, then Hans and Josef, then Geoff and I. Each time the water containers were brought back, they were immediately emptied for various uses and then taken by the next two. The guard looked to me to be more of a threat to himself than to us, but we nonetheless asked him politely if we could have a little water.

Following the playground rules, he then went to the post and returned a minute later to tell us that our request had been granted, but we must hurry. The droopy-faced little soldier, his oversized trousers dragging in the dust, sluffed behind us to the tap and stood about 10 feet off. After washing our faces and arms, we filled the containers, walked back to and out the gate.

Germans Call It Quits

We had not known what to expect at Bordji-Perez, and had hoped there would be some place for mechanical repairs, but since the fort and the hut were all there was, the Germans decided to throw in the towel.

Without new parts, the Volksbus was beyond hope. They would sort out what they needed and could carry, give us the remainder, and wait for the convoy to arrive and then continue south with it. It was a wise decision and the best to be made under the circumstances, but Geoff and I felt sad that they'd failed after all the hardship and bad luck. We agreed, though not eagerly, to take Hermann with us to Mali, where he would write or wire the families of the four fellows and tell them what had occurred.

That afternoon, Hans and I drove back to the Volksbus to bring it in. While he hammered the wheel on again, I loaded everything of ours and most of the heavy things from the Volksbus into the Rover, disregarding the spare tires from the roof rack, which Hans threw off, as well as a complete spare engine. We hitched the two vehicles together with the tow rope and started back to the post just as the sun was setting.

When we towed the Volksbus up to the front gate, the Arab came out and glanced at it disdainfully. Snatching the proffered passports from Hans, he counted them. We told him that three of us were leaving for Mali in a few minutes, and we needed our passports returned right away. He looked at me up and down, then sneered. They wouldn't be ready until 10 p.m., he sniffed. We would have to come back then. This time he strutted away without looking back. It didn't take much to work up a real hate for that fellow.

If the end of the Germans' vehicle had been a tragedy for them, it was certainly nothing of the sort for us. Our petrol supply had been three-quarters consumed by the time we reached Bordji-Perez, and without the 15 extra gallons we inherited from them, we had no possibility of reaching Gao. They also gave us a large box of tools: two hydraulic jacks, a tent, some food, and medicines, including the first malaria pills we'd seen. With the addition of these articles, we were equipped for Africa for the first time—except for visas, of course, and this was about to become a serious problem.

Until we entered Algeria at Beni-Ounif, we had not even considered the idea of needing visas for foreign countries. The very word "visa" implied to us some special circumstance or reason for entering a country that went beyond the simple motive of ordinary traveling. Our passports had allowed us into England, France, Spain,

Gibraltar, and Morocco without questions. We considered paying 14 dinars for visas when we arrived in Algeria to be an inconvenience more than anything else. After all, we were just tourists.

While some African nations were starting to encourage tourism, Mali was apparently not among that number. When Geoff inquired into Mali visas during his wait in Algiers, he was told that not only were Canadians barred from Mali without visas, but also that the necessary visas would cost $40 each, a small fortune in our circumstances.

He was also told of one party that had been refused admittance and turned back, despite their willingness to pay anything to be allowed to continue. They had to wait at Bordji-Perez for a week before a convoy came through with enough petrol to get them back to Reggane.

Despite this story, Geoff had decided that the visas were beyond our means and had returned without them. We had not been aware of a country named Mali before Gibraltar, and besides, $80 was too much to pay to cross a geographical entity we had no interest in, one that we had not come to see, and one we would pass through as quickly as possible. We decided to play the cards as they were dealt, working something out when the time came. Well, the time had now arrived.

THE POLITICS OF SUCCESS

Perhaps the most important and respected quality in people is what is called "social" or "emotional" intelligence. It is the ability to read other people in a complex situation, and then to speak and act effectively.

Political savvy requires understanding the dynamics of power and influence among people, and their responding appropriately to gain maximum advantage.

Of course, the time when political skill is most required is when you are angry, excited, or confused, when you are least likely to have your wits about you.

Your ability to think, plan, and act effectively will affect your success more than anything else.

CHAPTER 24

RUNNING THE BORDER

Late that afternoon, a truck came from Mali and stopped by the hut for the night. The driver was as interested in our story and the ruined Volksbus as we were in what he could tell us concerning the road ahead.

For a start, he told us, the road was quite bad, and he confirmed that if we didn't have visas we would not be allowed through. We asked him if, once we were past the border, there were any more checkpoints where visas would have to be produced.

There were, indeed. On the 350-mile stretch between Bordji-Perez and Gao, there were three towns, each having a police post to check traffic. He showed us his passport, with the stamps from each post, to lend credibility to his story, and assured us that it was impossible to pass without our passports, insurance, and visa registration in order. We listened intently to everything he told us, but laughed off his pessimism.

We were becoming reconciled to the sad fact that nothing in this trip was going to come easy. If it wasn't the Rover, it was the police, the dysentery, the heat, or the insects. There was always going to be something to make it rough until we got to Lagos. As usual, ***there was no question about turning back. It was onward or nothing.*** We would have to run the border, go around the checkpoints, and somehow get to Gao to secure enough petrol to get into Niger, the next country.

As foolish as we may have been, we appreciated the hazards of such a procedure. If we were caught in the country illegally, we could be imprisoned, indefinitely, and have everything we owned confiscated. It was not a pleasant prospect, but going back was worse. We would have to try it and just hope for the best. There remained nothing more to be said. We took down the addresses of our German friends and shook hands all around, wishing them good luck, and they us, each promising to look the others up should we ever be in their respective countries. We had converged, merged, and were now diverging on separate roads once more. Perhaps someday our paths would cross again.

At 10 p.m., we drove back to the main gate of the darkened fort to ask for our passports and fill our water containers. After 45 minutes and much confusion, we received our passports and water and left immediately for Tessalit, the frontier town of Mali, 75 miles to the south.

Even in the dark, as we drove toward Mali we could see and feel that the barren wasteland was falling behind us. There had been bits and tufts of withered grass in the rocky country around Bordji-Perez, and small clumps of sagebrush, and the lights of the Rover began to pick up stunted trees spaced haphazardly along the piste. The reappearance of the sparse vegetation was comforting in a way, seeming to stand as an assurance that nature, though not softening, would be willing to accede her position as our main antagonist, leaving the physical and political factors to create the difficulties for us to overcome, as the price we must pay for entering Africa unprepared.

We had never been so completely cut off from everything in our lives, with 1,000 miles of desert behind us and 1,000 miles of unknown country ahead, $50 in our pockets, and no clear reason why we were there to begin with. *This uncertainty generated a strange feeling of reckless determination with only one concrete objective that we could cling to and strive for—reaching Lagos, Nigeria.* We proceeded toward that town like the Wise Men following the star of Bethlehem.

THE DARING PLAN

Hermann rode between us, straddling the floor shift on the raised transmission. Since he had a Mali visa, he was only coming as far as the frontier, where he would wait until he could get another ride south the following day, or perhaps the day after. Traffic on that stretch of road was not too dependable.

Geoff and I had very little patience for Hermann. He had been nothing but self-righteous, meddlesome, lazy, and irritating. We were glad we wouldn't have to share his company any farther than Tessalit. We would leave him by the road if he started in on his holier-than-thou advice with us, and he sensed it. He sat quietly as we discussed the coming border running and what we could do in case of this or that eventuality. The first move would be fairly straightforward.

We would drive straight to the frontier town of Tessalit and deposit Hermann, taking a look at the lay of the land at the same time. We would then return in the direction of Bordji-Perez without even inquiring into entering without visas. Hermann would tell the police, who would undoubtedly be suspicious, that we were going to wait for the convoy and make the trip to Gao with the trucks from Bordji-Perez, and that he had been in a hurry and had paid us to bring him to Tessalit, where he hoped to find another ride. The story was flimsy, but it would serve the occasion.

After depositing Hermann, we would return along the road until out of sight of the frontier post, then turn west into the open country, beginning an arc that would bring us around the border and back to the piste about a mile beyond Tessalit. The road still ran more or less due south and with our compass to ascertain direction, we couldn't possibly get lost.

ONE HARD DRIVE

The truck driver had been right about the bad road. According to the map, it ran along the edge of a range of low rocky hills for the next 250 miles. Although it was still very much Sahara, the level sand had been replaced by a stony, broken terrain through which a track had been scraped, obviously at great cost in time and labor. No attempt had been made to keep the road in a reasonable state for the infrequent traffic—it being rife with gouges and potholes, narrowing to a few yards in many places, making any speed over 20 miles per hour dangerous and terribly hard on a vehicle. Realizing full well that there was no margin for error, we kept our speed down. If anything happened to the Rover now, the jig was up.

No one can appreciate the meaning of a hard drive until they have driven for many hours over really treacherous road. Geoff and I had been at the wheel for two days straight in our rambling trips across Canada and the States, and once I drove from Niagara Falls in the east to Vancouver in the west, a distance of over 3,000 miles, in 65 hours non-stop, alone. It took me 19 hours of solid sleep to get back on my feet. I was sure that nothing could be rougher than that.

But negotiating a buckled road, late on a moonless night, hundreds of miles from civilization, going into the fourth consecutive day without any sleep, having no idea of what to expect ahead—that was a "hard drive," beyond my wildest imaginings.

Driving the Land Rover was a process of maneuvering incessantly to avoid ruts and potholes, brooking no distraction whatever, the road just inside the sweep of headlights taking the focus of concentration, the eyes of the driver never leaving the road. Braking, shifting, accelerating, hands locked on either side of the wheel, shoulders hunched forward to absorb the crashing, pitch-

ing motion, peering intently through eyeballs fuzzy from strain—
that was a picture of the driver.

All of us were hunched forward, elbows on knees, eyes fixed
on the road to anticipate and prepare for the next jolt. We were
sweating from the taut nerves, gulping aspirins to relieve the
splitting headaches that were our legacy from the heat and sleep-
lessness. The only sensible thing to do was to stop for the night
and rest our weary bodies, continuing in the morning when we
had a little energy and could see the piste clearly, but we could-
n't. We couldn't stop at all, because it was now Sunday morning.

This was an important factor. Sunday was Sunday, even in Africa.
The chances that the Mali police would be less vigilant on a Sunday
were good, and if we were grasping at straws in our proposed course
of action, the tiniest straw had to be utilized.

FOUR TROUBLE SPOTS

To reach Gao without being stopped, we had to pass Tessalit,
then Aguelhok, Anefis, and Bourem. The four trouble spots were
spaced in distance, so that we could circumvent Tessalit in the dark
of early morning, Aquelhok just after dawn, Anefis in the midday
heat, and Bourem at dusk. In this manner, we would run the least
possible risk of detection by those police still working on Sunday.
After Tessalit, the advantage of being able to see where we were
going when we left the road was another consideration. It wasn't
much, as plans go, but it was all we had.

Hurdle 1. Half-obscured road markers kept us informed of our
proximity to Tessalit, and as the distance diminished, the tension
built. Just at 3 a.m., we passed several stone huts off to one side of
the road, and came seconds later to a barrier across the road with
the sign, "TEESALIT-ARRET POUR DOUANE." The road was
clear on one side of the barrier and without thinking, I swung the
wheel over and drove past it before stopping, dousing the lights
and cutting the engine simultaneously. The silence of the dark
night fell over us.

The police post, to our right about 20 yards, was completely
still. There was no sign of life anywhere.

"They must all be asleep," whispered Geoff nervously.

"Are you getting out or are you coming with us?" I asked
Hermann, also in a low voice. "Make up your mind," urged Geoff
tensely, "We're not staying here all bloody night."

The night was suddenly pierced by the angry barking of a dog,
coming from the same direction as the police building.

"I will come! I will come!" choked Hermann frantically.

I punched the starting button and released the clutch in the same motion, sending the darkened Rover tearing down the uneven road. After 100 yards of near-blind driving, I switched on the lights, stepping on the gas even harder and keeping it to the floor, despite the careening motion. It was five kilometers before I cut the engine and lights once more and coasted to a stop.

Geoff was already out and in back of the Rover when it stopped, and I joined him there, standing without a sound, staring into the dark toward Tessalit for any sign of pursuit. Five minutes of listening for any sound satisfied us that our passing had gone unnoticed. Cursing that damn dog, we started the engine again. The illegal crossing of Mali had begun.

If you can imagine a road constructed entirely of eight-inch diameter logs, packed closely together, then you can imagine the same road with countless logs removed and others spread out and broken irregularly. If you can then picture driving over this surface in a light vehicle with a solid frame, and the bone-jarring, teeth-rattling effect of it, you can have some idea of what it was like being a traveler in Northern Mali. Now add a dash of numbness, a touch of fear, two cups of exhaustion, a layer of tension, sprinkled with dust and grime, and you get the glorious sensation of traveling without visas in sub-Saharan Africa.

When the dawn came, we were bumping through a broken, jagged country strewn with black boulders. It looked like an abandoned graveyard of the devil. It was a cruel, unfeeling landscape, bits of scraggly sagebrush attesting to its ability to sustain only the barest forms of life. There was an air of silent violence hanging in the stillness, the rocky piste being the only sign that men had claimed a partial victory from the land. The piste was the only route a vehicle could possibly take, and according to the map, it led straight into Aguelhok.

Hurdle 2. We first saw Aguelhok that morning at 5:50, half an hour after sunrise, from a small hillock by the piste four kilometers out. It was a cluster of stone buildings facing what had been, hundreds of years before, a large lake. Now there was only a flat expanse of white sand bordered by small dunes, sparsely dotted with stunted, scrawny trees.

We examined the entire area from a boulder with binoculars, each of us taking a look. Our only way around the town was along the far perimeter of the old lakebed. We would still be in sight of the buildings, though over a mile away, but since it was still early morning, we hoped that no one would be looking.

It was a good bet. Shifting into four-wheel drive, Geoff steered the Rover along the lake edge, keeping as far from the quiet village as possible without getting into the powdery sand around the dunes. We were over halfway through the wide arc that would take us back to the road when the flat sand ran out. To follow the perimeter any farther would take us back toward town, so we took a chance in the silt. The wheels started to spin and churn immediately, slowing our forward motion to a crawl. The Rover slowly began to sink. Hermann and I jumped out quickly and put our backs into shoving while Geoff kept the wheels turning slowly. That was all it took; in another 50 yards of arduous straining we were through the dunes and curving back toward the piste, out of sight of the town.

We had no way of knowing if we'd been seen, so once we'd regained the road we drove for another five kilometers, then pulled off to listen and wait. Again we had been lucky. There was no sound of a pursuing vehicle from Aguelhok, and after 10 minutes, we backed onto the piste again and set out for Anaphors, 193 kilometers farther south.

Hurdle 3. The road still ran through parched, withered country, and although the dry, cracked ground was rocky, signs of life, in the form of ragged trees and bushes, were increasing with the miles. The sparse areas of greenery and trees were centered in the arid basins, singular to the lower Sahara regions, called wadis. A wadi is a shallow depression, like a huge dinner plate, usually several miles across, and so gradual in its slope to the center that unless one is aware of its existence, it is almost indiscernible. They are, however, one of the most dangerous physical features of that land, despite their innocent appearance.

Every two or three years, a rainstorm blows in from the Niger River, drenching the land in a sudden cloudburst before dissipating. Because the ground is baked solid after months under the pounding sun, the water from these infrequent storms is not absorbed, but runs into the centers of the natural depressions, the wadis, with frightening speed, filling the larger ones to a depth of 15 feet in a matter of minutes. Several travelers in that area, who had been passing unsuspectingly through a wadi when the storm broke, suffered the most cynical fate of nature—drowning in one of the driest lands on earth.

The French built their roads across the wadis on dikes of earth and stone, as high as 15 feet above the arid ground, so traveling was no longer dangerous, as in the old days. These land bridges look downright silly in their barren context, but the high-water mark, 12 feet up their sides, quells any tendency to laugh.

We passed no one on the roads that morning, and stopped only once to refuel and eat. Hermann managed to drag himself out and gather a little brush for our cookfire before wandering off to socialize with two Taureg children who had appeared in the scrub, standing about 20 yards off, eyes wide and sucking their fingers. As Hermann approached them, they vanished, only to reappear in another place, still watching silently. It amused us no end, Hermann's penchant for meeting people, and we agreed that he would make a perfect host for a boys camp on parents' day. Geoff and I were just too tired to care.

At noon the temperature was only 105 degrees, and at 1 p.m. when we were approaching Anefis, the mercury was touching 115 degrees—hot enough to keep most people inside, and too hot to drive safely, but we had no choice. We had to get while the getting was good. Scouting the terrain with the binoculars as before, we made another wide arc to avoid the eyes of the police in the small post. The uneven ground was blanketed by thin wispy grass and clumps of dry brush, but the terrain proved no obstacle to our Rover. Because of the flatness, we had to swing out about three kilometers, a time-consuming operation, and it was an hour before we safely circumvented Anefis and got back on the road. That left only Bourem between us and Gao.

THREE DOWN, ONE TO GO

Late that afternoon, we met a heavy truck going north. It was the first vehicle we'd seen since Bordji-Perez, 250 miles before, and we stopped to chat with the driver. After the usual pleasantries and a vigorous round of handshaking, the driver asked us if we had any Algerian money to sell. For some reason he seemed quite eager to buy it and offered us, what he swore to be, its equivalent in Mali francs. We still had 200 dinars (about $46) from Algeria and reluctantly agreed to part with half of it for 5,000 Mali francs.

At that time we had no knowledge of the black market and its influence on national currencies. We believed that you could change any money, from any country, in any large bank, for approximately what you paid for it. It wasn't until much later that we learned that in many countries the bank rate on foreign currencies is much lower than its actual value, and once you've changed your money, you're stuck with the foreign cash. You must either spend it all in that country, or exchange it on the black market when you leave. These same countries forbid import or export of their currencies, so they must be purchased through the bank, at the lower rates. After we left Algeria, our Algerian money became worthless to anyone but a person traveling to that country, and after that truck driver, we never met another such person.

The driving was rough on Geoff and me, but at least we had youth on our side, and were physically very fit from years of clean living and good sport. Hermann, on the other hand, was not strong. He was half bald, flabby, and completely unsuited for hardship. Yet, despite his physical shortcomings, and the terrible pounding he was suffering from the road, he refused to utter a word of complaint.

About 6 p.m., we stopped to refill the tank, not far from two goatskin tents set up in a gully between two mounds of sand. Hermann, his eyes glazed and his body dripping with sweat, struggled out of the back and fell on the road, prostrate and breathing heavily. Whether he lived or died was inconsequential to our getting past Bourem by dusk, and we paid no attention to him, beyond feeling a vague pity.

DESERT MIRAGE?

As I opened the tank and Geoff dragged out the last jerry cans, I had a sudden feeling of being watched and turned uncomfortably to examine the landscape. A flash of blue caught my eye from off to the right about 50 yards, and I forgot all about the tank and the semiconscious Hermann.

I then saw a Taureg girl, her bearing erect and proud, like a queen in exile, unafraid, almost defiant. She was simply beautiful, about 18 years old, with high cheekbones under a smooth olive skin setting off the dark, piercing eyes. Her jet-black hair, pulled tightly back on her head, was almost completely covered with a light blue scarf, long flowing folds of the same turquoise material embracing her slender figure. She stood perfectly still, watching us, half turned into the breeze that caused her robes to ripple in the afternoon sun, her arms hanging straight by her sides, relaxed, one bare, the other partially covered by a fold of the shimmering blue. There in the quiet of the day, against the background of sand and dusty bush, she looked like a delicate flower, and a shining jewel in an arid setting.

Geoff brought the jerry cans around and set them down, following my gaze without commenting, studying her lovely features as though she would vanish at any moment. She never flinched from our staring, never moved, never took her eyes off our faces. Finally she turned, as though satisfied, floated lightly across the sand, moved behind the tents, and was gone.

The spell was broken. We turned to the business at hand, and as I poured the last of the petrol out of the jerry can, Geoff helped Hermann to his feet and back into the Rover. When I started the engine, we both looked for the girl once more, but there was no sign of movement around the quiet tents. We drove away slowly, still looking, and were well down the piste before I stepped on the gas and shifted through the gears.

If there are things I am fated to remember always from that journey through Africa, surely one of them must be that Taureg girl in the lonely land below the Sahara.

The lesson is this: *Even in the remotest of places, you can happen upon the loveliest of creations. Like the delicate desert flowers, those apparitions appear and then vanish in a moment. You may think you have just seen a mirage, but no, it was real. And you are left to wonder about the miracle of life—and the magical moments of serendipity.*

BREAKING THE RULES

There are two types of rules: laws and conventions. Laws are passed by governments and enforced by police. Conventions are standard or common ways of thinking, only enforced by your natural tendency to do things the way they've always been done.

To succeed in a tough, competitive, fast-changing society, you have to be willing to defy convention, to try something new or different when the situation calls for it.

Sometimes the ideal solution is the opposite of what everyone else is doing. Often you have to offer something that is better, cheaper, newer, and more convenient than anyone else—all at once.

Be prepared to innovate, to break out of the mold, to "go boldly where no one has ever gone before."

Thomas Watson, Sr., founder of IBM, put it this way: "Do you want to succeed faster? Then double your rate of failure. Success lies on the far side of failure."

Or, as Dorothea Brand wrote, "Decide what you want and then act as if it were impossible to fail. And it shall be."

CHAPTER 25

A VERY CLOSE CALL

The crossroads at Bourem is shaped like a tree, the stem being the road on which we were driving, the road on the right leading northwest toward Timbuktu, and the one on the left going south toward Gao. To get onto the Gao road was a matter of approaching the crossroads, then turning off and cutting across the angle of which Bourem was the center. Then it would be just 59 miles to Gao.

Two hours before dusk, the terrain had become a sea of rolling dunes, with just enough silt in the sandy soil to sustain a covering of dark green, tangled clumps of narrow-leafed bush. The sun was touching the horizon when we came out of an S-bend onto a wide sandy expanse flowing half a mile, straight ahead, to the base of a looming hill. Crowning this hill, huge and shadowed by the setting sun, was the high-walled fort of Bourem.

In our condition, we were halfway across the open area before it registered on us that we were perfectly visible from the fort. A uniformed figure had already come out of a building at the base of the hill and was standing, hands on hips, watching our approach. I swung the wheel around and headed toward the road for Timbuktu, my heart thumping and stomach fluttering sickly.

A shout came from the uniformed figure and he started waving, motioning us in his direction, but I only increased speed to get away. Suddenly we hit a ridge of sand that tore the tailpipe loose from the muffler, bringing a deafening blare as we lurched onto the Timbuktu road and sped northeast out of sight of the fort.

If things weren't confusing enough with the policeman shouting at us from behind, the muffler roaring, and all of us trembling with fatigue and fear as we turned off the piste to circle back to the Tessaulit road, one of the tires started going flat on the front. Without stopping, we wended our way through the dunes until we came out on the road, crossing it into the sand hills beyond before cutting the engine. We had made a complete loop, and even if a vehicle had been sent in pursuit of us from the fort ahead, there would be no reason to suspect that we had turned off the Timbuktu road and had, in fact, regained and recrossed the same road on which we had appeared.

Working frantically, Geoff changed the flat tire while I removed both ends from a condensed milk can, split it down the seam, and bound it around the noisy break in the tailpipe, cinching it fast with spare radiator hose coupling. Our hearts were pounding a mile a minute, our mouths dry, and our hands sweating from the nearness of the escape.

We could have guessed that Bourem was a fort, but we had had no way of knowing that because of its strategic location the danger of detection was greater than it had ever been. We would now have to pass in the choppy country under the very eyes of the fort, and if we used our lights, the police would have no difficulty intercepting us. And the sun was now gone.

The lack of light in the unpredictable terrain was one problem, the loose tailpipe was another, since the muted sound traveled a long way, and our stumbling condition was yet a third. But we had no choice. We had to press on before the whole Mali army was down on us. In the murky afterlight of day, keeping the motor revs low, we started snaking our way through the dunes under the fort.

LIGHTS IN THE NIGHT

From the first, the sand was loose and treacherous, forcing us to use four-wheel drive to creep along the twisting, tortuous route. Unable to see clearly, we were steering in the general direction by keeping the looming fort always on the right. Soon, it was too dark to see anything, and so Hermann and I got out and floundered ahead with flashlights to find a way. Twice we got trapped in blind pockets and had to back out, pushing to keep the Rover moving in the clinging grit.

The one thing we had dreaded finally happened—we could see lights detaching from the fort and coming down the hill toward us, and when we cut the engine for a moment, we could hear voices shouting and see the lights spreading out as they moved. We were panic-stricken, sweating coldly and trembling all over. Keeping the lights off and ignoring the roar of the engine, Geoff stepped on the gas. The Rover churned forward, winding in and out in a switchback pattern toward the road somewhere ahead.

If each of those dozen lights represented a man with a weapon, our time was just about up, they being no more than 300 yards away, the bobbing line changing direction to follow the sound of the Rover. But the road couldn't be much farther, and the Rover was finally clawing its way ahead without our pushing. Running along with it, Hermann and I jumped back in just before Geoff roared it up over and down a large sand bank.

My heart stopped dead, and our jaws went slack with despair. Only 50 yards ahead the way was blocked with a semi-circular row of what appeared to be lanterns. The other lights were coming over the dunes to our right and behind us, and to the left was a steep ridge of brush backed by a clay bank. We were trapped.

"Go like hell and save your lights!" I shouted at Geoff, but he had already stomped on the gas, and the Rover surged forward. Five yards from the first light, he gave a blast on the horn and snapped on the headlamps, swerving to one side.

We almost died with relief at the sight. We were in the middle of a tent camp, heading for a row of cooking fires, while the frightened figures of running Tauregs streaked across the glaring beams, children being snatched frantically out of the way. Without slowing, Geoff steered toward a hole in the row of tents and we roared out of the camp. The Land Rover bounded along a wide footpath for another hundred yards, and suddenly we were on the Gao road.

Shoving the Rover out of four-wheel drive, Geoff wrenched the wheel over and once more opened up to full throttle, sending us lurching and bouncing down the rutted track. After 15 minutes of hammering along, we turned sharply off the road and parked 50 yards away, waiting tensely in the dark. After 10 agonizing minutes had ticked by, their passing marked by the relief of 20 hours of nerve-wracking tension, we knew we had made it. But, we had made it with nothing left—no smiles, no satisfaction, no strength, and no energy. It was as though a plug had been pulled, and the last drop of nervous energy—or whatever it was that kept us going— had drained away. We got back on the road for Gao and drove hypnotically, eyes blurred and heads ringing. Geoff finally stopped the Rover in the middle of an open stretch and slumped over the wheel.

"No use," he mumbled. "No use at all. I can't see any more. You'd better drive." A few miles later, I also gave up driving. The last shred of energy was gone, and I couldn't see the road clearly. I was dizzy, blind, driving down a flashing tunnel with hallucinations leaping and screaming from every shadow. Vaguely remembering the river to be on the right somewhere, I turned off the road and drove straight for it, until we came to the bank of a muddy tributary. Geoff and Hermann were slumped forward, almost unconscious, and as I stopped by a clump of palm trees, they jerked awake and looked around to see what had happened.

"We're there."

Without a word or question about the location of "there," we dragged the sleeping bags out of the rear and threw them on the ground. Then everything went black.

SECTION 7:
THE SUMMING UP—REFLECTIONS

You are wiser than you know. You have already had so many experiences in life that, if you extract from them every precious lesson, you could make your life into anything you want.

You must look upon every experience of your life as a building block, handed to you at the right time and place, just when you needed it to take the next step.

I said earlier that the key to success is for you to set a clear goal and then to persist through all adversity until you achieve that goal. The intense emotions of pride and self-esteem that accompany any great achievement will burn a pattern of success into your subconscious mind. Forever after, you will be internally motivated to repeat this pattern. You'll be set for life!

Take some time to analyze and evaluate your experiences. Write down the valuable lessons you have learned. Think about the wonderful things you have ahead of you.

And then, "Act boldly, and unseen forces will come to your aid."

CHAPTER 26

LESSONS FOR LIFE

We had made it! We had crossed the Sahara Desert. We had not really slept for four days, from Adrar far in the north to the banks of the Niger River. But we had done it. The first major test of our lives was over. And we had passed.

There was much more to come, but I won't go into that now. I won't tell how we eventually got out of the country of Mali and into Niger with an all-points bulletin out for us on all roads and with the army and police under orders to shoot to kill the "spies" and "arms smugglers" who had illegally entered the country and evaded all attempts at apprehension.

I won't go into everything that happened as we ran the next border illegally, evading police checkpoints, evading capture and traveling deeper and deeper into West Africa.

I won't go into the other countries we passed through and experiences we had, not even the time we spent with Dr. Albert Schweitzer at his hospital in Lamberene in Gabon. I won't relate the details of how we were almost killed under the boots and truncheons of Congolese police and how we escaped death to finally make our way to South Africa, our ultimate goal.

Instead, I'll end this story by telling you what I learned about life and success in the Sahara crossing.

SEVEN PRINCIPLES

Most success in life happens in retrospect, like looking in the rearview mirror to see what happened. Aristotle once wrote, "Wisdom is a combination of experience plus reflection."

When reflecting on your experiences, learn to extract the lessons and the wisdom that your experiences contain. People who merely have experiences but do not learn from them tend to make the same mistakes over and over. But, *if you have a single intense, important experience and you extract from it every lesson that it offers, you can often learn an extraordinary amount from it and use that new understanding to accomplish great things in the future.*

Here are seven principles you can apply to any challenge you face in achieving anything you desire.

1. The most important key to achieving great success in any endeavor is for you to decide upon your goal and then launch. Take action. Do something. Move! Your willingness to take the first step, to launch, to move forward toward your goal with no guarantee of success, is the critical step that separates the winners from the losers in life.

We set out at the ages of 20 with $300 each with a goal to cross North America from one side to the other, the entire Atlantic Ocean, the length of Europe from London to Gibraltar, and all of Africa, a distance of more than 17,000 miles—and we made it in 12 months. But the most important step was the first one. All the rest followed from that.

2. Once you've launched toward your goal, never consider the possibility of failure. The Germans have a saying, "Immer vorne, nie zuruck." Always forward, never backward. Never consider the possibility of failure.

Every person who achieves any success does so because he or she refuses to quit when the going gets rough. Your ability to persist in the face of setbacks and disappointment is the true measure of the person you really are, of the character you have developed.

Your persistence is your measure of belief in yourself and in your ultimate possibilities. Your willingness to persist is vital to all great achievement. And it is always a decision that you make personally, within your own heart. It is not what happens on the outside that counts. It is always what is happening on the inside.

3. The biggest goal in the world can be accomplished if you just take it "one oil barrel" at a time. Thomas Carlisle once wrote, "Our great business in life is not to see what lies dimly at a distance but to do what lies clearly at hand." The only time you will ever have is now, the present moment. It is what you do with this moment that determines your entire future. If you live every day, every hour, the best you can, the rest of your life will take care of itself. As the Bible says, "Sufficient unto the day are the cares thereof."

4. Avoid the naysayers. Watch out for the negative people around you who are always telling you that you will fail, that you will lose your time or your money, that you will "die in the desert." Associate with positive people. Get around men and women who are optimistic and ambitious. Refuse to listen to objections and reasons why you can't succeed. Remember, if every possible objection must first be overcome, nothing will ever get done.

5. Welcome obstacles and difficulties as valuable and inevitable steps on the ladder of success. Remember that difficulties come not to obstruct, but to instruct. Within every difficulty or setback lies the seed of an equal or greater opportunity or benefit. Your job is to find it. Our trip to Africa was one problem after another. We ran out of money over and over again. We strained every muscle of our bodies trying to ride bicycles across France and Spain. Our Land Rover broke down again and again. We suffered from dysentery, heatstroke, and exhaustion. But when it was time, we were ready for the Sahara crossing. Without the lessons that we had learned from our mistakes, we would surely have died in the desert. And when you look back on any great achievement, you will find that it was preceded by many difficulties and many lessons. The difficulties are the price that you pay for your success—and no success is possible without them.

6. Be clear about your goal but be flexible about the process of achieving it. Be willing to change, to try something new. Keep your mind open and fluid and flexible. Be willing to accept feedback from your environment and correct your course. This is a key quality of peak performers. They are not rigid; they are flexible. They are willing to consider the possibility that they could be wrong. It's not what they have, but what they do with what they have that separates the winners from the losers in life. It is not what happens to you, but how you respond to what happens to you that counts. Your response to the adversities of life is the real measure of who you are and what you are made of.

The Greek philosopher Epictetus once said, "Circumstances do not make the man; they merely reveal him to himself." You find out who you really are when you face a great adversity or disappointment and you are tempted to quit and to go back. This is the true test. And the only question is whether you will pass or fail. The decision is always up to you.

7. Nobody does it alone. At every step of the way on our journey, people helped us with advice, with food, with assistance, and with money, but especially with warmth and kindness and generosity. Likewise, at every turning point in your life, someone will be standing there with an outstretched hand, offering advice or assistance or an encouraging word.

We never forgot the kind people who helped us in our trek across France and Spain—nor the people in Gibraltar who helped us prepare for Africa. We won't forget the mechanics in Morocco and Algeria who helped us with our repairs. We will never forget the generosity of Monsieur Tourneau of Michelin who gave us that precious map that saved our lives when we were deep in the desert.

When life is over, we will treasure most the memories of the people with whom we lived and laughed and loved. These are the true components of wealth—the true accomplishments of our journey.

So don't be afraid to ask others for help. It is a mark of strength and courage and character. And don't be reluctant to give of yourself to others generously. It's the mark of caring and compassion, and personal greatness.

The reason the Sahara crossing was so life-changing for me was because after the Sahara, I never felt that there was anything I could not do. I felt programmed for success for life, although it took me many years to understand what had really happened.

I believe that *everyone has a Sahara to cross,* perhaps more than one. You may be crossing your own personal Sahara right now.

Everyone goes through periods of great difficulty—their own private hells, their dark nights of the soul—but by facing whatever life gives you with courage and determination, you grow more surely toward the stars.

Let me end this story with the last verse of "Carry On":

> *There are some who drift out in the deserts of doubt,*
> *And some who in brutishness wallow,*
> *There are others I know who in piety go*
> *Because of a heaven to follow.*
> *But to labor with zest and to give of your best,*
> *For the sweetness and joy of the giving,*
> *To help folks along with a hand and a song,*
> *Why there's the real joy of living!*
>
> *Carry on! Carry on! Fight the good fight and true;*
> *Believe in your mission, greet life with a cheer;*
> *There's big work to do, and that's why you are here.*
> *Carry on! Carry on! Let the world be the better for you;*
> *And at last when you die, let this be your cry:*
> *Carry on, my soul! Carry on!*

If you resolve that whatever life hands you, you will carry on, there is nothing that can stop you from achieving the greatness for which you were created.

BECOMING UNSTOPPABLE

"Nothing in the world can take the place of persistence. Talent will not; nothing is more common than unsuccessful men with talent. Genius will not; unrewarded genius is almost a proverb. Education will not; the world is full of educated derelicts. Persistence and determination alone are omnipotent." **Calvin Coolidge**

"Before success comes in any man's life, he is sure to meet with much temporary defeat, and perhaps some failure. When defeat overtakes a man, the easiest and most logical thing to do is to quit. That is exactly what the majority of men do." **Napoleon Hill**

"Some men give up their designs when they have almost reached the goal; while others obtain a victory by exerting, at the last moment, more vigorous efforts than ever before." **Heredotus**

"Austere perseverance, harsh and continuous, rarely fails of its purpose, for its silent power grows irresistibly greater with time." **Johann Wolfgang von Goethe**

"Few things are impossible to diligence and skill. Great works are performed not by strength, but by perseverance." **Samuel Johnson**

"Never, never, never give up." **Winston Churchill**

"Our greatest glory is not in never falling, but in rising every time we fall." **Confucius**

"There is no failure except in no longer trying. There is no defeat from within, no insurmountable barriers, save our own inherent weakness of purpose." **Elbert Hubbard**

"The rewards for those who persevere far exceed the pain that must precede the victory." **Ted W. Engstrom**

"The most essential factor is persistence, the determination never to allow your energy or enthusiasm to be dampened by the discouragement that must inevitably come." **James Whitcomb Riley**

"If you can force your heart and nerve and sinew to serve your needs long after they are gone, And so hold on when there is nothing in you, except the Will that says to them, 'Hold on!'" **Rudyard Kipling**

"I know of no such unquestionable badge and mark of a sovereign mind as that of tenacity of purpose . . ." **Ralph Waldo Emerson**

"No, there is no failure for the man who realizes his power, who never knows when he is beaten; there is no failure for the determined endeavor; the unconquerable will. There is no failure for the man who gets up every time he falls, who rebounds like a rubber ball, who persists when everyone else gives up, who pushes on when everyone else turns back." **Orison Swett Marden**

"Do what you can, with what you have, right where you are." **Theodore Roosevelt**

"Always bear in mind that your own resolution to succeed is more important than any other one thing." **Abraham Lincoln**

"A man can rise above his circumstances and achieve whatever he sets his mind to, if he exercises unshakable persistence and a positive mental attitude." **Samuel Smiles**

"Many men fail because they quit too soon. Men lose faith when the signs are against them. They do not have the courage to hold on, to keep fighting in spite of that which seems insurmountable. If more of us would strike out and attempt the 'impossible,' we very soon would find the truth of that old saying that nothing is impossible. Abolish fear, and you can accomplish anything you wish." **Dr. C. E. Welch**

"Men who have blazed new paths for civilization have always been precedent breakers. It is ever the man who believes in his own ideas; who can think and act without a crowd to back him; who is not afraid to stand alone; who is bold, original, resourceful; who has the courage to go where others have never been, to do what others have never done, who accomplishes things, who leaves a mark on his times. Don't wait for extraordinary opportunities. Seize common ones, and make them great." **Orison Swett Marden**

"Nothing can resist a human will that will state even its existence on its stated purpose. The secret to success is constancy of purpose." **Benjamin Disraeli**

"I am not discouraged, because every wrong attempt discarded is another step forward." **Thomas Edison**

"We will either find a way or make one." **Hannibal**

"Life is either a daring adventure or nothing." **Helen Keller**

"Experience is not what happens to a man; it is what a man does with what happens to him." **Aldous Huxley**

"Obstacles are necessary for success because victory comes only after many struggles and countless defeats. Each struggle, each defeat, sharpens your skills and strengths, your courage and your endurance, your ability and your confidence—and thus each obstacle is a comrade-in-arms, forcing you to become better." **Og Mandino**

"To get profits without risk, experience without danger, and reward without work is as impossible as it is to live without being born." **A. P. Gouthey**

"You must be courageous, and courage is the capacity to go from failure to failure without losing any enthusiasm." **Winston Churchill**

"The credit belongs to the man who is actually in the arena; whose face is marred by dust and sweat and blood; who strives valiantly; who errs and comes short again and again; who knows the great enthusiasms, the great devotions, and spends himself on a worthy cause; who at the best knows in the end the triumph of high achievement; and who at the worst, if he fails, at least fails while daring greatly." **Theodore Roosevelt**

"It's easy to cry that you are beaten and die; It's easy to craw-fish and crawl; But to fight and to fight when hope's out of sight; why, that's the best game of them all." **Robert W. Service**

"Courage is resistance to fear, mastery of fear—not absence of fear." **Mark Twain**

"Nothing splendid has ever been achieved except by those who dared believe that something inside of them was superior to circumstance." **Bruce Martin**

"Do not pray for tasks equal to your powers. Pray for powers equal to your task." **Phillips Brooks**

Carry On

It's easy to fight when everything's right,
When you're mad with the thrill and glory.
It's easy to cheer when victory is near
And wallow in fields that are gory.
It's a different song when everything's wrong,
When you're feeling infernally mortal.
When it's ten against one and hope there is none,
Buck up little soldier and chortle,

Carry on, carry on! There isn't much punch in your blow
You're glaring and staring and hitting out blind,
You're muddy and bloody but never you mind,
Carry on, carry on. You haven't the ghost of a show.
It's looking like death, but while you've a breath,
Carry on, my son, carry on.

And so in the strife of the battle of life
It's easy to fight when you're winning;
It's easy to slave, and starve and be brave,
When the dawn of success is beginning.
But the man who can meet despair and defeat
With a cheer, there's a man of God's choosing;
The man who can fight to Heaven's own height
Is the man who can fight when he's losing.

Carry on, carry on. Things never were looming so black;
But show that you haven't a cowardly streak,
And though you're unlucky, you never are weak.
Carry on! Brace up for another attack.
It's looking like hell, but you never can tell.
Carry on, old man! Carry on!

There are some who drift out in the deserts of doubt,
And some who in brutishness wallow,
There are others I know who in piety go
Because of a heaven to follow.
But to labor with zest and to give of your best,
For the sweetness and joy of the giving,
To help folks along with a hand and a song,
Why there's the real joy of living!

Carry on! Carry on! Fight the good fight and true;
Believe in your mission, greet life with a cheer;
There's big work to do, and that's why you are here.
Carry on! Carry on! Let the world be the better for you;
And at last when you die, let this be your cry:
Carry on, my soul! Carry on!

—Robert W. Service

About Brian Tracy

Brian Tracy is one of America's leading authorities on human potential and personal effectiveness, and chairman of Brian Tracy International, a human resources company based in San Diego, California, with affiliates throughout North America and in 31 nations worldwide. He has had successful careers in sales and marketing, investments, real estate development and syndication, importation, distribution, and management consulting, and he has consulted at high levels with many billion-dollar-plus corporations.

As an internationally renowned business consultant and motivational speaker, Brian addresses over half a million people each year on leadership, management, sales, strategic planning, success, personal and career development, goals, time management, creativity, self-esteem, and other topics. His exciting talks and seminars bring about immediate changes and long-term results. He is a dynamic and entertaining speaker with a wonderful ability to inform and inspire audiences toward peak performance and higher levels of achievement.

Brian has produced and narrated many best-selling audio and video learning programs, including *The Psychology of Achievement, Fast Track to Business Success, The Psychology of Selling, Peak Performance Woman, The Psychology of Success* and *24 Techniques for Closing the Sale.* These programs (over 30 in all) were researched and developed through over 25 years, and are some of the most effective learning tools in the world. They cover the entire spectrum of human and corporate performance. Brian is also author of several best-selling books, including *Maximum Achievement* and *Advanced Selling Strategies.*

Brian has traveled or worked in over 80 countries on five continents and speaks four languages. He enjoys a wide range of interests and has earned a bachelors degree in commerce and a masters degree in business administration, as well as a black belt in Shotokan Karate. He is extremely well-read and regularly studies management, philosophy, economics, metaphysics, and history. An avid believer in controlling one's own destiny, setting daily goals, working hard, and persevering to the end, Brian believes "If it's worth doing, it's worth doing poorly at first."

He lives near San Diego, California, with his wife, Barbara, and their four children.

ABOUT BRIAN TRACY INTERNATIONAL

Brian Tracy is one of the most popular and exciting speakers in the world. His fast-moving, high-content delivery—including humor, ideas, insights, and practical strategies for greater personal and professional effectiveness—makes him one of the most sought-after speakers in the U.S. and around the world. In the past 20 years, he has delivered more than 2,000 speeches, seminars, and courses for more than one million people.

Brian is available to corporations, associations, conventions, and public seminars on the following topics:

High-Performance Leadership—For the 21st Century
Advanced Selling Skills—For the Top Professional
Time Empowerment—To Double Your Results
Maximum Achievement—To Get the Most out of Life
Sales and Service Excellence—To Keep Customers for Life
Superior Sales Management—To Build World-Class Teams

Each presentation may be customized and personalized for clients. For rates and availability please contact:

Brian Tracy International
462 Stevens Avenue, Suite 202
Solana Beach, CA 92075
phone: (619) 481-2977
fax: (619) 481-2445
e-mail: braintracy@briantracy.com
website: www.briantracy.com

In the U.S., call toll free: **1-800-542-4252.**

To receive more information, or to order any of these exciting, life-changing programs, please call Brian Tracy International at 1-800-542-4252.

1. The Psychology of Achievement: *(6 audiotapes and workbook)*
Perhaps the most powerful personal improvement program ever produced. Take charge of your life, set and achieve goals, and unlock your super-conscious mind. *$60.00*

2. The Psychology of Success: *(6 audiotapes)*
Discover the 10 proven principles for winning with this amazingly comprehensive program. Listen today—you'll see results tomorrow! *$60.00*

3. Master Strategies for Higher Achievement: *(6 audiotapes)*
Think and act better and faster. Increase your personal value and personal fortune. More than 150 key ideas to use immediately. *$60.00*

4. How to Start and Succeed in Your Own Business: *(6 audiotapes)*
Double or triple your profits with this mini-MBA course. Learn key requirements for business success, strategic marketing, corporate strategy, and how to overcome the challenges of leadership. *$60.00*

5. The Psychology of Selling: *(6 audiotapes and workbook)*
Put yourself in the top 10 percent of all salespeople. This is the best-selling audio program on selling in the world: available in 14 languages in 31 countries. It works! *$70.00*

6. The Universal Laws of Success and Achievement: *(8 audiotapes and workbook)*
Discover 153 of the most powerful and important laws of success, achievement, happiness, wealth-building, selling, and negotiating in all of human history. *$80.00*

7. How to Master Your Time: *(6 audiotapes)*
Gain at least two hours every day! Overcome procrastination and maximize your productivity—and, most important, find out why time management is life management. *$60.00*

8. Thinking Big—The Keys to Personal Power and Maximum Performance: *(6 audiotapes)*
Tap into the vast resources of your mind, unlock your unlimited potential. Practice the ideas in this program and you will become unstoppable! *$60.00*

9. The Science of Self-Confidence: *(6 audiotapes)*
Learn how to develop unshakable self-confidence. Learn the keys of persuading and how to deal with difficult people. Plus: how to become fearless in your work and personal life. *$60.00*

10. Accelerated Learning Techniques: *(6 audiotapes, 96-page workbook, plus one bonus audio)*
Learn how to memorize quickly, speed-read, improve your brainpower, and multiply your intelligence. *$60.00*

11. Getting Rich In America: *(6 audiotapes)*
You can achieve financial independence! Learn easy-to-follow methods that have helped thousands of men and women reach financial independence. *$60.00*

12. How Leaders Lead: *(6 audiotapes and workbook)*
Together with Ken Blanchard, Brian explains the importance of vision, courage, integrity, and much more. Establish key result areas and develop the "Winning Edge!" *$80.00*

13. Advanced Selling Techniques: *(6 audiotapes, workbook)*
Learn about GAP analysis, risk management, relationship selling, and much more! Discover what the future holds for your successful sales career with this groundbreaking program! *$70.00*

14. The Luck Factor: *(6 audiotapes)*
Luck is predictable. Learn the skills you need to experience higher levels of success and satisfaction in all areas of your life. *$60.00*

15. Breaking the Success Barrier: *(6 audiotapes)*
By mastering the easy-to-learn principles in Brian's newest program, you will actually make your life easier, cut your workload in half, and dramatically increase your energy and stamina. *$60.00*

16. Peak Performance Woman: *(6 audiotapes)*
Principles, techniques, and key methods to enable any woman to get ahead rapidly in her career and personal life. *$60.00*

17. How to Raise Happy, Healthy, Self-Confident Children: *(6 audiotapes)*
Discover the four behaviors of effective, joyful parents. Learn what you can do to help your child feel he or she is a special part of your family. *$60.00*

18. Success Secrets of Self-Made Millionaires: *(1 audiotape, 1 videotape, workbook)*
Discover the 21 qualities that have rocketed self-made millionaires to the top—qualities you won't have to learn the hard way. *$95.00*

19. Creative Job Search—Over 101 Ideas on How to Get and Keep the Job You Really Want: *(1 audiotape, 1 videotape, workbook)*
Take control! Benefit from 50 years of research into creative job search. Find a better job, greater opportunities, and higher salaries by following these ten steps. *$95.00*

20. How You Can Start, Build, Manage or Turnaround Any Business: *(8 audiotapes, workbook)*
Over 500 ideas you can use to increase profits, boost sales, cut costs, and improve performance in every area of your business. *$195.00*

21. The Management Advantage: *(12 audiotapes, workbook)*
Brian Tracy, Tom Peters, and 41 top management experts bring you 12 solid hours of practical ideas you can use to be more effective in every part of your business life. *$150.00*

22. Action Strategies for Personal Achievement: *(12 two-cassette audio volumes, action planner, goal planner, and index)*
This program is the accumulation of Brian Tracy's 25 years of expertise in studying professional achievement, personal happiness, and wealth building. *$180.00*

Executive Excellence

Since 1984, *Executive Excellence* has provided business leaders and managers with the best and latest thinking on leadership development, managerial effectiveness, and organizational productivity. Each issue is filled with insights and answers from top business executives, trainers, and consultants—information you won't find in any other publication.

"Excellent! This is one of the finest newsletters I've seen in the field."
—Tom Peters, co-author of *In Search of Excellence*

"Executive Excellence is the Harvard Business Review *in* USA Today *format."*
—Stephen R. Covey, author of *The 7 Habits of Highly Effective People*

"Executive Excellence is the best executive advisory newsletter anywhere in the world—it's just a matter of time before a lot more people find that out."
—Ken Blanchard, co-author of *The One-Minute Manager*

CONTRIBUTING EDITORS INCLUDE

Brian Tracy

Stephen R. Covey

Ken Blanchard

Marjorie Blanchard

Charles Garfield

Peter Senge

Gifford Pinchot

Elizabeth Pinchot

Warren Bennis

Denis Waitley

For more information about *Executive Excellence* or *Personal Excellence*, or for information regarding books, audio tapes, CD-ROMs, custom editions, reprints, and other products, please call

Executive Excellence Publishing at:

1-800-304-9782

or visit our web site: **http://www.eep.com**